T0067910

# Simultaneously In Existence

## FROM A POET'S VIEW

ROBERTA BLANGO

Order this book online at www.trafford.com
or email orders@trafford.com

Most Trafford titles are also available at major online book retailers.

Print information available on the last page.

ISBN: 978-1-6987-1338-0 (sc)
ISBN: 978-1-6987-1337-3 (e)

*Trafford rev.  11/16/2022*

www.trafford.com

North America & international
toll-free: 844-688-6899 (USA & Canada)
fax: 812 355 4082

# Acknowledgements

I must first thank my Almighty God for giving me this special gift of writing poetry. It's a privilege to be able to share my forth book with all of you. I hope you thoroughly enjoy it.

I would like to thank my children, grandkids, and my family for their continued support throughout my book-publishing journey.

I would like to thank my editor, Ann Hedrick, for doing an awesome job editing my book.

I would like to thank Trafford for accepting my third manuscript. I would also like to thank everyone on the production team, with a special thanks to Eve Ardell and Josh Laluna for keeping me abreast of each step throughout the production process. Thank you for allowing me to incorporate some of my ideas with the design of my book. I couldn't be happier with the amazing finished product.

Keep God first in your life and He will always make a way for you to thrive as long as you are alive!

# Contents

### We've All Been Betrayed

### We've All Been Encouraged

### We've All Been In Relationships

## We've All Been Lonely

## We've All Been Thankful

## We All Befriend

## We All Love Our Families

### We All Experience Happiness

### We All Experience Mother Nature

### We All Have Self-Confidence

### We've All Encountered Life Experiences

## We've All Felt Angry

## We've All Felt Hopelessness

## We've All Felt Proud

## We All Have Dreams & Talents

## We All Have Regrets

## We All Need Alone Time

## We've All Been In Love

## We All Stress

## We All Suffer From Heartbreak

## We've All Experienced Sadness

We've All

B

e

e

n

Betrayed

# Betrayed

*B*etrayal stings the soul
And leaves people acting cold
No matter what age young or old

The kind of pill that's hard to swallow
Leaves your insides hollow

Destroys trust
Hearts crushed
But getting on with life is a must

You cry and cry
Want to die

They smile in your face
And stab you in the back
Is how a betrayer act

You don't find out until it's too late
And your love
Has now turned to hate

Betrayers hurt people with their unforgivable lies
And they make it hard for the next
Gals and guys

Roberta Blango

# Beware of Those U Think U Know

*I* thought I knew my best friend well
Until she stole my man and told me to go to hell

Could I have been that naïve
Her actions were hard to conceive

Friends since the age of ten
Went on double dates with all our men

We shared everything
She jeopardized a 20-year friendship
Over a fling

She got him for one night
And then he told her to take a hike

She got exactly what she deserved
Then came crying to me, she had a nerve

I can forgive her, but I'll never forget
Her betrayal almost made us split

Our friendship will never be the same
With friends like her, who need enemies
It was a valuable lesson learned
Trust is not given, it's earned

# In The Dark

You'd rather hide behind me
Then face the truth
Sorry, it's time to let them know
Know who you are
The real you
The one that hides
Behind the drugs and booze
Because of whom you choose
To be with in the dark
But it's time for it to come to light
Honesty is the key
So stop deceiving me and relieve me
Let me go
You play your role well
Have everyone fooled
Except me
I see it in your eyes
You can't disguise them from me
Live your life free
Stop pretending to care
Just to avoid the stares
Because you're not being fair
To me

# No Trust Left

It's a shame when you feel as though you can't trust anyone
Due to the corrupt things that are done
Having no trust for anyone is no fun

The only one I feel as though I can really trust is the Lord
He will never let you down
A true friend indeed
That meets every need

People will stab you in the back so quick
Therefore be careful of the friends you pick
People are so sly
Leaving you in torment asking yourself why

Wanting to know what you ever did to them
You come to realize it was all just a game
A part of their twisted scheme
Some people are just pure mean

That's why in this day and time
I trust only Jesus, and me, myself, and I
When I meet people
I'll greet them with a simple
Hi and good-bye

Times have changed
People only care about themselves
They will lie and deceive
Just to get ahead and achieve
It's sometimes hard to conceive

But this is how it is
Stay alert and know
When people are being polite or
Pretending to be your friend
It could all just be for show

Live longer
Laugh harder
Just be a little smarter

# Some People Will Do Anything

People will do and say anything
To get their way
Lie, cheat, and steal
It's no big deal
It comes without a conscience
At will

Heart cold as ice
Fake and act nice
Stab you in the back
And not think twice

There are no limits
To their slickness
Will blindside you
With the quickness

Can't be trusted
Will deny they did wrong
Even when they get busted

"All that glitters
Is not gold"
These folks have no soul
And will try to take control

You usually find out too late
After you've taken their bait
Then you start to hate
Telling yourself this couldn't
Have been your fate

Just be aware
Of folks faking like they care
A snake in the grass
Is hard to detect
So run for your life
If you suspect
Or
You'll be their victim
Next

# You Compulsive Liar

You lie, lie, lie,
Until the day you die
That's why I'm telling you good-bye

Lies roll off your tongue and out of your mouth with ease
Uncontrollable like an incurable disease
You'll say anything to fulfill your selfish needs

You're no wolf
A snake in sheep's clothing is who you are
Lies won't get you very far

What happened to love, honor, and respect?
Morals you surely neglect
One of the main reasons we could never connect

You tell lies so well it comes natural
No effort needed
If telling lies was a career
You would have successfully succeeded

There's no trust
Nothing else left to discuss
Getting away from you is a must

Another lesson learned
Anyone can get burned
From a compulsive liar
Whom you blindly desired
Knowing deep down inside
He never had the qualities you required
That would take your life higher

When you take risks
You may end up pissed
From a liar like this

We've All

B

e

e

n

Encouraged

# Be a Dad Regardless

*Y*ou might not be ready for the baby you helped create
But you chose to act irresponsible
Therefore, you must start being responsible
Because this life you created didn't ask to be here

Now you're angry because she doesn't want to murder your child
Listen to yourself, you'd rather kill
Are you for real
What's the deal?
With these deadbeat dads
You should have asked if she was taking her birth control pills

This child is a part of you too
Your blood running through its veins
So stop being lame
And live up to your name

A name that will be passed on to your offspring
How can you look into those precious eyes?
And not want to be a part of their life
Even if you don't want their mom for your wife

Dads, stop neglecting your kids
Love them regardless
To avoid a lifetime of pain
This child will endure
Wanting to know who you are and your name

They may seem ok
But deep down within there's an empty place
Them imagining your face
Wanting your genuine embrace

Do the best you can
Your best is better than nothing at all
They'll be willing to take whatever they can
Because to them, you'll always be their dad
Not just any ole man

# Be Grateful

*O*nce your treasures have been snatched
There's no getting them back
Throwing your life all off track
Being grateful for what you have
Will reflect what you think you lack

Everybody seems to want more
More of this
More of that
Never satisfied with what they've got

I like that old saying
"Someone is always doing worse off than you"
Wishing and praying they could fulfill your shoes
And willing and able to do what you do
So yes,
We should all be a little more grateful it's true

Need to prioritize
Then maybe you could optimize
It's okay to upgrade
With the hard earned money you've made

Just remember to keep things in perspective
Then being grateful will be effective
We all want and deserve nice things
Without the hardship they sometimes bring

Sometimes your wants must wait
Until a later pay date
Remember
As long as you get it
It's never too late

*Roberta Blango*

Having something
Is always better
Then having nothing
So be grateful and blessed
Is what I'm trying to express
Because you could have less

# Chop It Up

Don't let scornful people still your joy
Chop up their mean ways and soar
Don't give them the reactions they crave for
Learn to ignore

Smile at them instead
That will mess with their head
Throw them off guard with a positive glow
Let them know
You're running the show

If we all learn to chop up negativity
There would be nothing in the world
But positivity
And that's reality

Carrying it around
Brings you down
Leaving your face
Full of unattractive frowns
Looking like a circus clown

The next time someone or something
Imposes upon your happiness
Taking away your bliss
Simply dismiss
Continue to persist
As though they or it doesn't exist

# Comes A Time

Comes a time to stand your ground
Comes a time to retaliate without making a sound

Comes a time to live your life right
Comes a time to overcome your fright
Comes a time to embrace the starlight
Starting tonight

Comes a time to move on
Comes a time to ignore your scorn
Comes a time to be reborn
Comes a time to patch up what's torn

Comes a time to lead
Comes a time to intercede
Comes a time to share what you believe
Comes a time to rescue instead of flee
Comes a time to influence the young breed

Comes a time to grow up
Comes a time to stir up
Comes a time to dish the fairy cup
And measure up
Comes a time to shut up and step up
And strut your stuff

Comes a time, comes many times
For life's improvements
Life's amendments
Life's developments
Life's advancements
Life's adjustments
Life's perfections

That may or may not need correcting
Due to someone or something intersecting

Comes a time when there will be the unexpected
Leading you in an unforeseen direction
Of your mirrored life reflection!

# Do Your Thang

You took the next step
Now get ready
For whatever lies ahead
Positive or negative, there'll be no turning back

This is just the beginning
To a magnificent ending
Of the messages you're sending

People enjoy what you have to say
About life situations of today
Reassuring them everything's gonna be okay

Don't stop
Until you reach the top

Take the good with the bad
Never let them see you get mad

Represent God's favor
With a twist of your flavor
For them to savor

Some will like
Some will not
Just do your best
And show them
What you've got

# God's Willing

*W*hen God's willing
Many things can and will happen for you
Through your faith He'll grant it too
This is nothing new
Every word is true

There will always be skeptics
Who don't believe
Until they've seen it achieved
But God will make you a believer
And become a Bible reader

**Ask**
It shall be given you
**Seek**
Ye shall find
**Knock**
The door shall be opened unto you
A scripture from the Bible …..Matthew 7:7

As simple as ……..
One, two, three
Now do you believe me
Only God can set your
Mind, body, and soul free

He keeps his promises
Never leads you astray
Just continue to pray
Each and every day
He'll show you the way

He'll change your life around
Without making a sound
No other like him to be found
He wears the ultimate crown

He'll always have your back
Pick up where you slack
Keeping track
Of the devil's attacks

An awesome God He is indeed
To provide our every need
Helping us to succeed
And will continue to concede
As long as you believe
And keep the faith
I guarantee

# Good Things Happen

Good things happen to those who wait
A sign from God
Letting you know it's never too late
When it comes to fate

Keep faith present
And what was meant
No one can prevent

Once it's in your cards
From the good Lord
You're sure to get your reward

Never give up on your dream
Even if things aren't peaches and cream
Because the Lord
Can turn around even the extreme

He can handle anything
Keep him first
And your life will soon reverse
Released from the bad luck curse

Treasures at the end of the rainbow
To let you know
He's always there
Never going to let go
Wants to see your smile glow

Happy ever after
With joy and laughter
Due to the good things
Our **Awesome God** brings

*Roberta Blango*

# His Powerful Hands

The Lord's mighty hands
Upon this great land
More powerful than any man

Unstoppable!
Uncontrollable!
Unchangeable!
But extremely lovable!

Healing
Saving
Providing grace
All over the place
At his own pace
To assist us in the heavenly race

Bibles provided to help us understand
His master plan
Nothing more or less
Than to attest
To his greatness

Always an ear call away
Each and every day
To listen to what we have to say

How incredible is it
To have a God so exquisite
Don't be afraid to admit it

With us for life
More committed
Then any husband or wife

One of a kind indeed
To fulfill our needs
And will always succeed

Don't miss out
Learn for yourself what He's about
And you'll soon become a believer
Without a doubt

Our God's mighty hands here to protect
Not neglect
But to try to keep us in check
With a conscious mind
So in the end
None of us
Will be left behind

# Integrity

What does this word mean to you
What do you want it to mean to you
Do you want to make it mean something to you

Try it today
Try it without delay
Then apply it each and everyday

You will discover a person full of
Honesty
Sincerity
Morality
Righteousness
Completeness
Will you be able to handle all of this
It's the only ethical way to exist

Who are you without it
Where will you go in life without it
What will you accomplish without it
How would you survive without it

It represents and defines who you are
It will take you far
Make you as popular as a star

You'll receive the upmost respect
You'll be selected for number one projects
Your future perfect
As long as you stay in check

Never let success go to your head
A choice you will ultimately dread
So stay true to yourself instead

There will be no regrets
There will be no unpaid debts

Integrity is the best way to live life whole
And to acquire all your dreams and goals

# Lips Zipped

Keep your lips zipped
If you don't want people to flip

Over something you said
That got misled
Or, some rumor spread
Avoid it by keeping your lips zipped instead

If you don't have anything nice to say
Continue on your merry way
And try to enjoy the remainder of your day

You never know who's near
Whose ears
Hear
The words you smear

You shouldn't go around hurting people's feelings
It's unappealing

You never know what people are going through
Then have to deal with immature people like you
Making them feel blue
They need you to zip your lips
If they didn't ask for your point of view

There's a valuable lesson to be learned
Start acting concerned
If you don't want the same treatment in return

# Satisfy You

*Y*ou must be satisfied with yourself
Before you can satisfy someone else

If you're not happy with you
You're not going to be happy with another

You'll continue to harbor that bitter soul within you
You must change that person you're unhappy with

Or be alone until it no longer exists
You'll continue to fail if you persist

No one will ever be able to satisfy you
No matter what they try to do
Because you're not being true

Not sharing the way you really feel
Always keeping it concealed
Like a dangerous weapon

Protecting your heart
Protecting your soul
Being ice cold

Only you have the power
To release what ails you
A burden you have no desire to share
Thinking no one would care

Getting it out will satisfy you
Becoming that person you never knew

*Roberta Blango*

The one that's been hiding all these years
The one afraid to appear
The one that wanted no one near
The one that never wanted to hear

Now you're the one that sees things
Crystal clear
Because you finally faced your fears

# Tender Heart

Tender heart pumping strong
All day long
Even when it's being treated wrong

Want to protect it
Want to comfort it
Want to rest it
Want the Lord to bless it

Want people to treat it right
Even though it's out of sight
Respect it with all your might

Take care of it
And it will take care of you
It depends on what you choose to do
Of how far it will take you

Love can bring it joy
Love can also destroy
The heart of any girl or boy
Therefore, be cautious once you start to explore
What the world has in store

Everyone you come across is not your friend
Although they will pretend
Until the very end

Many things in life may or may not
Shatter your heart into pieces
But if so …………..
Put it back together again
Jump start it
Pump it harder than before
The heart is delicate but it's also very strong
And it's not to be ignored

Roberta Blango

# The Love of God

Unconditionally
Is the best way
To describe
Our Heavenly Father's
LOVE
Sacrificed His only Son
To forgive us of our sinful ways
He deserves our nightly praise
No one can compare
It seems unfair
But that's just how much
He truly cares
For you and me
Until the day we die
Not one selfish bone
Which is why
He sits on the highest throne
Everyone should be proud
To call Him their own
Prince of peace
His love never decreases
Constantly increases
Day to day
As He awakes us
With His loving **Grace**
Place to place
Such a blessing
To have someone
Love us so much
Our Lord and Savior, Jesus Christ, the Almighty and Powerful
One hundred percent unconditional love
Straight from up above

# Turn the Other Cheek

You must learn to turn the other cheek
Don't get upset if someone doesn't speak
Don't let petty stuff ruin your week

When someone does you wrong
The experience should make you strong
Shake it off, instead of worrying all yearlong

When someone doesn't pay back
Although it maybe whack
It's not worth stressing over, having a heart attack

Feeling betrayed
Felt you got played
Don't let the pain inside be displayed
Never let them see your joyful spirit fade
You deserved that promotion
Don't show your emotions
It's not worth causing a commotion
And ending up with a demotion

Someone jumped in front of you while in line
Knowing they were behind
You want to curse them out, but be kind
They're just testing your state of mind

Customer got a bad attitude
Acting all rude
Don't come unglued
Remain calm and smooth

Your significant other wants to fuss and fight
Tell them not tonight
And he or she is going to be alright
And then display a smile that's big and bright

You'll win every time by turning the other cheek
Because it's a mind over matter technique

# Wise Up

$\mathcal{W}$ise one wise one
Open up your eyes
Stop listening to the lies

Close your ears
Until they disappear
Along with your fears
Then go the tears

Don't want to believe
How the closest ones deceive
Until the facts are retrieved

Your conscience is usually right
When problems are not displayed in plain sight
Wise up and see the light

You have the power
To turn a situation around
When it becomes sour

You may seem weak
It's a mind game
Open your mouth and speak
Stop accepting the blame

Be brave
Be strong
Be yourself

You're too smart
Too wise
And intelligent
To continue falling
For the same old lies

*Roberta Blango*

Time to discover
A new you
An improved you
That can handle
Whatever life decide to
Throw at you

# Your Worth

Value your worth
Don't be demeaned by another
Poisoning your mind thinking you're worthless
Always tell yourself
You're just as important as the rest

No one can put a price on your worth
You're priceless
One of a kind
Straight from the Lord's design

People can be so harsh
Their words can sting down to your inner core
There's no answer for
The way some people destroy
Just have to learn to ignore

Respecting yourself is most essential
Because you have the potential
To do whatever
Your heart desires
With that mind frame
You're sure to go higher and higher

Never quit
Must have that go-getter spirit
Words of advice can take you far
Being worthy doesn't mean
You have to be a superstar
Just be who you are

Don't become hypnotized by another's worth
Thinking you must live up to their standards
Create your own way
Take charge today

A person can tear you down
If you don't stand your ground
Speak up when need be
Or you'll be left feeling empty

Your worth
From birth
Is valuable until the day you die
Don't let another tell you differently
No matter how hard they try
Because the Lord made you
That's why!

We've All

B

e

e

n

In Relationships

# Bad Relationships

*A* relationship can be hard work
Especially when your better half acts like a jerk

The person you thought you knew so well
Taking you through pure hell
Love turned stale

You start thinking what went wrong
Why are they hanging out all night long
Leaving you all alone

Endless fussing and fighting
Nothing left exciting
A relationship now so uninviting

Don't know which way to turn
When the other is acting unconcerned
This time you got burned
But it's a lesson well-learned

All cried out
No more tears left
Too drained to shout

So stressed and depressed
Starting to care less
You tried your best

Love is a two-way street
It will never work if one
Decides to cheat

Once the trust is gone
The love fades away fast
And your relationship becomes
A thing of the past

# Be With the One You Want

I can't be someone else
I'm me
Not this fantasy person
You want me to be

Why did you ask me out?
If you had doubts
What was that all about?
Now constant flaws
Being pointed out

Don't like this
Don't like that
Want me to get rid of this
Want me to look more like that
I'm too fat
Constantly laughed at

My brain is fried
You've taken away my pride
Now I stay inside
Trying to hide

Believing all this crap
You keep filling my head with
Making me feel trapped

Before I met you
I was happy with me
Just as I am

You need to leave
Go find this person
You're trying to create
I'm getting out of this relationship
Before it's too late

You've done enough damage
To my self esteem
But now my soul has been redeemed
Now when I look in the mirror
I no longer feel ashamed

If you can't love me the way I am
Then scram

Never allow another to change who you are
Loving yourself will take you far

# Can We Make Up

*I*'ll forgive you
And please forgive me
Because this isn't the way
Two lovers should be

I want you and only you
And I hope you feel the same way too
I'm tired of what we're putting ourselves through

Let's forget about the past
And make our love last

We've done each other wrong
Now let's make it right
Starting tonight

You're my soulmate
We've known this since our first date
Cupid's arrow didn't make a mistake
I want you back now, I can no longer wait

I'll beg and plea
If that'll make you listen to me

I miss you
I need you
I love you
You know it's true

Commitment is the key
Trust is a must
For two hearts that've been crushed

A new start is what we need
To proceed
Glad we both agreed

It will be just us two forever this time around
Because we're standing on common ground
As I approach the alter in my beautiful wedding gown

*Roberta Blango*

# Don't Get Hooked Too Fast

Getting attached too soon is a mistake
You need time to determine if your relationship is real or fake

A new relationship always feels good
Like it should

If you want it to last take it slow
And get to know
The person who has you wearing a glow

If it's meant to be
It will be
But be patient and wait and see

When you rush
You're guaranteed to get crushed

Go out, have fun
But go home alone when you're done

He/she will respect you more
And is sure to adore
This special person whom he/she has been waiting for

# Go or Stay

Do you want me to go or stay?
Please give me one good reason
To try and make this work another day

Back and forth like a yoyo
Want you back, want you to go
Confused don't really know

Which way to turn
Scared of getting burned
But for your love I still yearn
But your infidelity has me concerned

Even if I decide to let go
I'll continue to love you till the day I die
Although I keep asking myself why

You cheat like there's no tomorrow
Causing constant grief and sorrow

You say you only love me
How can that be?
With all the other women you see

I can't take this anymore
I'm leaving
Not to get even
To end all the deceiving

You weren't ready to commit
So we must split
It's just hard for you to admit

Bye, hope you are happy now
I made my decision to go
But I'll always love you though

# Here We Go Again

Around and around I go like a merry-go-ride
Still confused, can't decide
If I want to leave or remain by your side

You've hurt me so many times it's not funny
Then you expect me to forgive you when you say, sorry honey

I'm getting sick and tired of your repetitious lies
My love for you was blind, but now I've opened my eyes

And I see you for who you really are
An enemy and we're at war

Telling me you love me, while at the same time getting smack
Like a fool I continue to take you back

I'm about to abort this ride
Because you're like Dr. Jekyll and Mr. Hyde
You can never say I haven't tried

The time has come for me to say **Goodbye**
And find me a decent guy

# I Want You Close

*I* want you close to me
I want you to hold me tight
I want to lie in your arms every night

Protecting me from harm
You'll be my safety alarm
All I need is your strong arms

Forever hugging and loving me
Just me
Forever **Me**

Till death do us part
Heart to heart
Never to depart

Unconditionally is the way
To forever obey
The words we recited at the altar
On our wedding day

Love you today
Love you tomorrow
Love you for eternity
The way everlasting love
Was meant to be

# Ice Veins

Ice must flow through your veins
Because your actions are insane
Don't care how much pain
You inflict
Once you're ticked

Mouth foul
Personality split
It's like watching a horror flick
You're acting out the crazy person's skit
And then the next day
You pretend you didn't do it

Saying I'm exaggerating
I need a tape recorder
Or camcorder
So you can see how disordered
Your mind gets
When you snap

It's not normal behavior
You need the Lord and Savior
To calm you down
And bring you back around
To common ground

Getting professional help
Should be our next step
Due to the memory loss
Before you come across
The wrong person

You're colder than ice
Eyes alone will slice
A person in two without using a device
You were once nice
Now you don't think twice
Please consider taking my advice
Whatever the price

*Roberta Blango*

# I'm Not Your Enemy

All I want from you is love
Unconditional love
Love me, don't hurt me
I'm not your enemy

Can you say those three words
Soft and kind
Not harsh and cold
And mean it
I'm not your enemy

Want to be with you for life
Love being your wife
I need you to complete me
I'm not your enemy

Don't ask for much
Just your gentle touch
Why hurt your loving queen
Treating me mean
I'm not your enemy

A love so strong
Can't be wrong
Share your pain
I'm here for you
I'm not your enemy

Cherish what you have
Don't push my love away
Say what you need to say
I'll understand
I love you
I'm not your enemy
So please open up to me
And set your soul **Free!**

# Know Your Mate

Get to know your date
Before deciding they're your soulmate
And discovering another side of him/her too late

Take your time
Be patient
Don't rush
Before your heart ends up crushed

Make sure their kindness isn't just a front
Ask about their past
Ask about their family
If there's nothing to hide, he/she should answer fast

If they hesitate
Or start to get agitated
That's a sign, they're hiding something, end it quick, don't wait

You don't want to get trapped
By his/her slick sly rap
Filling your heart with a bunch of crap

The end results won't be nice
From a guy or gal with a heart cold as ice
Disguised in sheep's clothing, making you think twice

Love at first sight
Sometimes blinds the heart from receiving
The warning light
Of the person you've just met and fell in love with overnight
Just because he/she was polite

*Roberta Blango*

Love takes time
Love takes commitment
Love takes patience
Love takes communicating
Love takes a lot of getting to know one another
Before going to the altar and saying I do to each other

# Naïve or Stupid

Some women are naïve
Others are just stupid

Evidence in plain sight
Constantly fuss and fight
Each and every night
Need to make him disappear
Faster than the speed of light

Covers his tracks
With frequent contact
To avoid the impact
Of you finding out the facts
Of his deceiving acts

Undercover brother
Don't want to disappoint his mother
Disguises his lovers
While going out of town on frequent travel
To be with the others

Disappearing act
Never around
Can't be found
Got you on a merry go round
Then come home putting you down
Whenever his feet finally touches your ground

Punches you in the face
Doesn't matter the place
Constant disgrace
Always wanting to pack your suitcase
Kids make you stay

To endure repeated abuse everyday
Listening to his lies
Telling you everything is going to be okay

Ladies, run, run, run
This can't be fun
Before you break
And come undone
With a 45 caliber **Gun!**

# What Do You Want

Do you want to be in a relationship with
someone treating you like crap?
Or be alone and happy taking peaceful naps

Do you want someone who stays out all times of the night?
Or do you want to live worry-free without this useless person in sight

Do you want to be sad and miserable all your life?
Or find your true soulmate and become his/her husband or wife

Do you want to be with someone that doesn't really love you?
Or find someone who deserves you

Do you want to be with someone who doesn't help with the bills?
Or do bad by yourself and chill

Do you want to be with someone who cheats?
Or be with someone who's honest and sweet

Do you want to be with someone who hits?
Or are you going to split

What are you going to do?
Go or stay
Let him/her continue treating you this away
Or go and live the rest of your life stress-free starting today

# Wish He Could See What I See

His love
My nightmare
My baby loves her
This I can no longer bear

Wish I could break the love spell
I've tried and failed
Hope I never hear wedding bells
That would be a life of hell

He's blinded by her looks
Girl can't even cook
And don't even mention books

Wish my baby would wake up and see the light
See that I was right
Without her interfering
He'd have a future successful and bright

She's not the one
She's not even fun
Wish I could somehow persuade my son

Have to let him live his life
Have to let him choose his wife
Even if it causes strife

Hope he doesn't wake up too late
And decide to choose her for his mate
That would be the saddest date
He would no longer be able to escape

We've All

B

e

e

n

Lonely

# How Long Should I Wait

How long should I wait
For my soulmate
Before it's too late

Age not on my side
Whoever said patience is virtue, lied
I need me a man by my side

I've waited long enough
Living a single life is rough
Ignoring all the happy couples has been tough

I'm ready for companionship
I'm ready for someone to hold me tight
And kiss me goodnight

I'm ready to give love a try
He's either going to make me happy
Or make me cry
But I want to experience something
Before I die

Tired of being home alone
No one to talk to on the phone
No one to call my own

I'm going to start online
That's how my best friend found hers
Maybe that's how I'll find mine

I'm going to wait no more
It's my time to explore
I'm no longer going to ignore
What my mind, body, and soul
Have been craving for

# I Miss

*I* haven't had a warm touch or gentle kiss in a while
Haven't found the right one
Haven't been treated like a special queen
I've been removed from the dating scene

I missed all the attention
I missed having fun
I missed having my name mentioned
I feel like my time is done

Will I ever find my soulmate
Or is it too late
Or should I continue to wait
I'm a procrastinator which I hate

I want true love one day
I want things to turn out the right way
I want to hear him say
He wants me in his life to stay

Bestow my heart
Help me chose smart
So no one will rip it apart
Protect it like fine art

I'm ready to give it a chance
I'm ready for romance
Someone to make me laugh
And take me out to dance
It's time for my life to enhance

Because
**I miss**
The gentleness of a sweet kiss
And my life filled with bliss

We've All

B

e

e

n

Thankful

# Another Year "2016"

*I* survived another year
Thanks to my Heavenly Father's countless blessings
I'm still here

Grateful to be alive
Because I could have died
If He didn't place His Angels
By my doctor's side

Another year
To spend with family and friends
And my lovely grands

Who bring me so much joy
What more could I ask for
Just thankful for each and every day
To get to see them play

I have my New Year's resolutions
This year they won't be just an illusion
Due to better choices I'll be choosing
Staying positive will be the ultimate solution

I'm going to work harder to make this a better year
Improving my life with a little cheer
Getting out more
And stop being a bore

Don't know what 2016 will bring
Don't know if I'll be accepting my engagement ring
Don't know if I'll see another summer, winter, fall, or spring
At this point I don't know anything
That'll be determined by my
Heavenly King

# Falling Dream

As I descend
My mind spins
In circles
Circling around
Before I reach the ground
Fright ignites
Imagining the sight
It's going to be when I land
Contemplating the impact
Instant death
Or suffering the repercussions
Could I survive?
Such a dive
Would I want to?
No quality of life
Or maybe luck on my side
And I continue to thrive
Lucky to be alive
Seconds before the fatality
Reality awakens me
From my horrible dream
Right before I was about to scream
My eyes opened wide
I jump up out of bed
Stumbling in darkness trying to reach the bathroom
To wipe the sweat from my forehead
Thanking the Lord
I'm alive and not dead

# Paradise

*W*onder what's paradise like?
Full of life's desires
The kind that keeps you inspired

Is it a happy place?
Full of laughter and grace
All stress and depression erased
Forever from your face

Is it like in my dreams?
Everyone friendly no one mean
And acting insane
A place where no one complains

Is it the most beautiful place in the world?
Like a sea of pearls
One day I'd like to give paradise a whirl

Pretend or not
My imagination
Is where it will all begin
And prepare me to start
Living once again
In my own skin
Paradise
Will surely welcome me in

It will be a dream come true
A life I never knew
A place that will help me get through
A phase of feeling blue
**Paradise!**
I can't wait to visit you

# Sent From Up Above

*I* truly believe this man was sent
From up above
For me to love

He and I clicked right away
We still reminisce of our first encounter
Still today

The magic in our eyes
Told us the feeling we shared
Couldn't be lies
Been married for five years
My how time flies

Nothing or no one can interfere
When the love you have for one another is true
It's up to you what you choose to do

We chose to honor and trust
Save the lust among just us
Faithfulness is a must

This is the only way to make your marriage last
If you don't abide by the rules
It will end fast
All the love you once shared
Will be a thing of the past

So don't take the risk
Jeopardizing the true love you've found

There's no better feeling
Knowing the person you're with will always be around
Until you're both six feet underground

# Wonderfully Made

We are all wonderfully made
By our Lord and Savior
From afar
So be proud of who you are

Form the strands of hair on top of your head
To the nails on your toes
Every inch of your body
Was uniquely composed
And is what our good Lord chose

We are created in different
Colors, shapes, and sizes
There's no need to try to revise
Your lips, nose, or eyes
He gifted you to your parents
The world's greatest prize

For some that's still not enough
They tend to add or get rid of stuff
Some will never be pleased
Due to relentless bullying and being teased
Changing their looks becomes an obsession
From the years of angered feelings they've been suppressing

Nevertheless, we should all be grateful
For Him blessing us with life
Regardless of unforeseen strife

You're here
Wonderfully made
Don't let others diminish your worth
As long as the Lord allows you to remain on earth

# We All

## Befriend

# Always Here for You

*Y*ou can always count on me my friend
When trouble in your life ascends

I'll be here when you need an ear
This offer is from my heart and sincere

Tears from pain
Tears of joy
Tears over a no-good boy
Pick up the phone and call
That's what a good friend is for

I'm here for you today
I'm here to stay
I'm here until the pain or
Whatever ails you goes away

I'll try to uplift your spirits the best way I can
I'll be there to lend a helping hand
I'll be the one who will always understand

You and I, friends forever
Depart never
Here for you for eternity
Through every endeavor

# Fake Friends

It is always that one that reaches deep within
That fake and pretend to be your special friend

I'm too old to play games
And will quickly refrain
Not going to let it affect my self-esteem

Life certainly goes on
No matter where you are from
Please do not stay and be dumb

Sometimes it is too good to be true
There is only a lucky few
That escapes what these fake friends put you through

Just another lesson learned
It was just my turn
To finally get burned

I'll do what I do best
I don't know about the rest
But I could really care less

Moving on to the next and not stress
Will complete my test

This is real life
Sliced like a knife
And filled with strife

Won't let it get me down
Or wear a permanent frown
Just wasn't intended for me this time around

# Loyal Friends

Friends come a dime a dozen
But a loyal friend comes into your life
Every blue moon

The kind that will stand by your side
And never leave you to deal with difficulties on your own
And will always lend an ear any time day or
night when they hear your voice
On the phone

Friends come and go
But a loyal friend will never let go

Make a loyal friend mad
They won't talk about you behind your back
They'll confront you and let you know
They won't hold a grudge
They are quick to let it go
To keep the friendship afloat

A loyal friend feels your pain
And you feel theirs
And that's how your strong bond remains
And will sustain the test of time
Even when family, friends, and outsiders
Try to intervene

Value your loyal friends
Treasure them until the end
Treat them with the upmost respect
And don't take advantage of what you have
Because once it's gone
You are going to be full of regret
Not having that special person to lean on

*Roberta Blango*

# Miss You Friend

*I* feel abandoned
Have no one to talk to
No one to hang out with
What am I to do?

Lonely and sad
Depressed and mad
Lost the only friend I had

Now I'm lost
Don't know which way to turn
Have no one to be concerned

A good friend is so hard to find
Disappointed that I no longer have mine
Some friendships are hard to leave behind

Especially over something petty and dumb
Makes my insides numb
Treasure your friendship, is the rule of thumb

I know I'll find another
But this one was like no other
Our type of bond is hard to discover

Maybe one day I'll get it back
And we will get back on track
Because I miss her and that's a fact
The next time I'll be more careful how I react

I miss you friend
And I can't wait until you're back in my life again

# My Friend

My friend, my friend
What are you going through?
Share whatever's on your mind, and
Peace you'll find

I know you, like the back of my hand
You know whatever it is, I'll understand

You are my best friend
When you hurt, I hurt as well
You're holding something deep within,
I can tell

Your eyes are sad
Your words are few
Your expression is blank
Your body restless
Please, tell me what it is
So you'll be stressed less

I've always been there for you
That's what a best friend chooses to do
I want to release you from this burden inside
That you try, but cannot hide
My friend, let go of your pride

I don't care how big or small it may be
Your secret will always be safe with me

You are torturing yourself so immensely
You are making yourself sick
Getting this off your chest
Will heal you quick

I'll be here waiting whenever you're ready to share
Because my friend,
I love you and I care

# Must Bite Your Tongue

$S$ometimes in life
You must bite your tongue
Hold back your frustrations
Although it's often hard to do
When someone is trying to get over on you

You have to shake it off
And keep on moving
And not let them know they have gotten
Under your skin
When you see them, politely grin

Don't give them the satisfaction
Of thinking they have won
By having you come undone

People you think you know
Are so low
The mean ones will stab you in the back
Throwing your friendship off track

You live and learn
Even the closest ones will burn
People will say and do anything
To make it to the top
And won't stop
At any cost
Even a friendship lost

When you confront them
They're looking dumb
They are the worse kind
The ones you need to leave behind

*Roberta Blango*

Release the built-up anger from within
Regain your composure
Count to ten
Bite your tongue
And try to start over again
With a trustworthy friend

# Never Thought It Would End

Never thought a friendship like ours would end
I thought we were best friends
Guess it was just all pretend

Once so close
Now a feeling of loss

Blindsided
Didn't see it coming
Never thought it would come

We used to have so much fun
Never imagined we'd come undone

Life is so strange
So many twists and turns
You live and you learn

Nothing's set in stone
Secrets of the unknown
Leaving you feeling blown
And disowned

Life goes on
What's done is done
It wasn't meant to be
Now I clearly see

Must bury what we had
Although it makes me sad
Even a little mad
Disappointed to be exact
But I'd never ask for it back

It would never be the same
The shell games
Now serving a different team
What a shame

I miss what we had long ago
But I'm going to let it go
Goes to show
You really don't know
Who you think you know
Until you've dealt a low blow
And get to know
A side you never wanted to know

# Thought You Were My Friend

*I*'m at my wits' end
I don't have the strength to go through this again
Fake friends pretending to be a friend

Stab you before you turn your back
Putting on an act

Like everything is fine
I should have recognized the signs

Giggling at every word that escaped his mouth
When he didn't say anything to make her laugh

A dirty sneaky snake in the grass
Beware of those wearing a mask

The friendly disguise
Right before your eyes
Dumb, but think they're wise

This is déjà vu
A squashed friendship way overdue
I pray it doesn't happen to you

If so, end it as quick as you can
Or they are sure to try and steal your man
Again and again

# You Say You're My Friend

*I*f you are my friend
You would know I hate when you play games
Stop communication between us
Just because you're going through something

If you are my friend
You would know I suck at remembering to call
You should be there to keep me on my toes and on the ball

If you are my friend
You would know I'll always have your back
Through thick and thin

If you are my friend
You would know I can be trusted one hundred percent
I've always loaned my shoulder when you needed to vent

If you are my friend
Why would you stab me in the back
With friends like you, I don't need enemies
I now realize you were never truly my friend
I'm going on with my life
And I'm not looking back
I don't want your friendship
If **this** is how you are going to act

We All

L

o

v

e

Our Families

# Handful Of Joy

Can I have a handful of joy?
To bring on good cheer
While my loved ones are here

To visit for a short time
Then return to their homes
From the cities they are from

Such a joyous occasion
Having them here
Year after year

Lots of reminiscing and laugher
And eating Thanksgiving dinner after
Will certainly miss them once they are gone

The only times we get together
Is on special holidays
Next is Christmas
My turn to hit the road

Favorite time of the year
Having family near
Everyone so sincere
Couldn't ask for a better atmosphere

Love surrounding the room
Grandpa and Grandma
Father and Mother
Brother and Sister
Cousins and Grands

All together holding hands
That is all the joy I'll be needing

# Her Father's Love

*A*ll she ever wanted was her father's love
But it was his son he always put above

She did everything to get his attention
Not once were the words, "I love you" mentioned

His son could rob, steal, and even kill
And her father would act as though it was no big deal

All she wanted was his affection
And to feel he would be there for her protection
But all she ever received was his rejection

This made her so mad
She started acting out and being bad

She started searching for his love in other guys
Thinking that would fulfill her inner desires

He never put her first
And things only got worse

One day she asked him why
His answer made her cry

He said, he "never wanted a girl"
That was the most devastating news in the world

How could a father deny his child because of her gender
She knew she could always depend on her mom to defend her

She grew up and became a beautiful dove
But it meant nothing without her father's precious love

# Must Keep In Contact

Keep in close contact with the ones you love
To show them you love them and you care
And will always be there

Doesn't matter who
Family, friends, or an old love, it's up to you
As long as you understand my point of view

A loved one can be here today
And gone tomorrow
Leaving your heart filled with sorrow

Pick up the phone, write a letter, or take a quick trip
Don't neglect your loved ones
Making them feel disowned and all alone

It's never too late to catch up
Even if it's been a while
It's nothing like reminiscing about old times
To bring upon an unexpected smile
Take time to make that call
Write that letter
Take that trip
It will definitely be worthwhile

Express yourself as often as you can
Be your loved ones biggest fan
Keeping in touch
Doesn't take much
Stop using petty excuses as a crutch

Live today
Love today
Never let it fade away
Keep it on replay

# My Grandson

Jamod, your precious face brightens up my day
You turn my sour days sweet
By kissing your soft chubby cheeks

Thank You Lord for sending this little boy
To love, cherish, and adore
Although your powerful kicks are starting to make
Grandma a little sore

I love the way you smile so hard when you see me
It is an indescribable feeling from deep within
Only another grandparent could relate
Being your grandma feels great

I love you just as you are
Wouldn't change a thing
I love your adorable little slobbery face
You could never be replaced

You are my first grandbaby
Although you may not be my last
I am going to value my time with you
Because you're growing so very fast

I'm going to be here for you until the end
You're my little cuddly bear
With a cute dimple and sandy brown hair

Cookie is the nickname I gave to you
You are only four months old
The perfect age for your grandma
To snuggle with and hold

# My Son the Artist

*H*is artwork is outstanding
And his artistic ideas are forever expanding
An art career is what he is planning

He can draw anything he wants to
You'll be astounded by what he can do

He has been drawing ever since he was a small child
And I'm so very proud

He's going to become a pro
I'm just letting you know
I'm going to be the first to attend his art show

He's truly blessed
Leaving viewers impressed
By doing his best

He's going to college to learn even more
There is so much in life to explore
And he's eager to learn about it for sure

No one taught him, he learned on his own
Spending hours on his drawings in his room alone

I know he is going to succeed
He was born to lead
And it's going to happen if he continues to proceed

He is a special young man and is going to go far
He's always going to be my **Superstar**
Son, yes you are!

Roberta Blango

# New Life (My daughter's first pregnancy)

There is a new life growing inside
A new life making my stomach wide
That I'm unable to hide

A nine month wait
For my delivery date
The part I hate
Hope I'm on time, not late

Tummy so round
My weight up and down
Feet can't be found

Heartbeat so strong
Sonogram can't be wrong
My son now 10 inches long

I got my boy
To bring me joy
He was worth waiting for

His precious little face
Lit up the entire place
Can't wait to give him his first embrace

It is an indescribable feeling
A new life coming out squealing
Waiting for the love I will be giving

An instant bond from the start
Heart to heart
Never to depart

# We All

E
x
p
e
r
i
e
n
c
e

## Happiness

# Anything U Want

*I* don't mind catering to a man like you
I love the things you do
Continue to treat me like a queen
I'll serve you for life
Whatever you want
Anytime you want it
House clean
Dinner hot
Bathwater ran
Massage
Your wish is my command
Keep a permanent smile upon your face
Never stressed
Plenty of rest
Treat you like a **King**
All winter, fall, summer, and spring
You will never want for anything
A man like you is hard to find
Therefore I don't mind catering to you
Because you are one of a kind

# Christmas Time

*A* time when family and friends come together once a year
Far or near
To talk, laugh, eat, and spread cheer
Creating a happy atmosphere

Houses decorated so nice
Making strangers turn and look twice
Presents under the Christmas tree
For your loved ones
Who wait anxiously

A time when love, joy, and peace are increased
And are shared
By the ones who love you and care

A time when no one should be alone
A time when extra love should be shown
A time when good deeds are not a loan
A time to let go of grudges and atone
A time to embrace the unknown
A time when beautiful snow is falling depending on where you are
A time to relax with a hot cup of cocoa or tea
While admiring all your creativity
Such an awesome sight to see

Christmas songs on every radio station
To get and keep you in the mood
With a positive attitude
While you serve your family their food

Christmas
The birthday of Jesus Christ
Who paid the price
With his life
So that you and I may live
The ultimate sacrifice

There is no better gift that can ever be given
So when you commit a sin
Please don't forget to ask to be forgiven
And learn to treasure the life you are living

*Roberta Blango*

# Sad Tears Turned Into Joy

Tears now of joy
Because of you boy
Releasing my pain
Replacing it with a smile
Something I haven't seen in a while

You made me believe in love again
Thought it was permanently erased from my brain
Since you have come into my life
Nothing has been the same
Thank you for asking for my name

A day I will never forget
The day my life turned around
Erasing all my frowns
With sweet whispers of your gentle sounds

No more screaming and shouting
And constantly pouting
Wished I'd met you a long time ago
When my life was sooo low
But you're here now though

Never thought I would ever experience love like this
Thought it had passed me by
Thought I would never meet the perfect guy
Until that blissful day you walked by
And now happy tears I cry

I had to pinch myself
Didn't think you were real
My past had stolen my thrill to feel
You coming along was so surreal

You mended my broken heart
Gently replacing it part by part
Like a work of art
Closing that chapter
To begin a fresh start

Thank you for making me believe in love again
Thank you for taking it slow giving me time to heal
Thank you for making me **Want** to live
Thank you for turning my sad tears into joy
I'll love you forever more
You were definitely worth waiting for
I Love You Boy!!

We All

E
x
p
e
r
i
e
n
c
e

Mother Nature

# Aging

Aging is a stage of our life
Some are okay with it, some are not
But it is one thing we cannot stop

Young then old, is our life's cycle
Here today, gone tomorrow
And the earth continues to rotate
No one can escape

Face wrinkled
Bones brittle
Hair thinning
Mother Nature seems to be winning

You have no choice but to cope the best way you can
It affects both women and men

Life goes on and on
From generation to generation
Since creation

Age with pride
Take it in stride
But it is something you cannot hide

Live your life with no regrets
Welcome your old age
Think of it as a new chapter page
And you are playing as a new character on stage

You only get better with time
Be blessed you were given God's gift
To live to see an old age
And stop acting like it is a crime

# Our Creatures

As I stare up at the mountains so high
I see large eagles fly
While low in the valley
Creepy bugs crawl by

Where are they going?
Do they belong?
Or are they all alone

Nature has been a mystery
All throughout history

We study them
Do they study us?

What if they do
What if they wanted
To get to know you

Would you be willing?
Or would it give you an uneasy feeling

We don't give them a choice
Because they don't have a voice

So they try to escape
When they sense or see a human's shape

Wouldn't want to be in their shoes
Not having a choice to refuse
Getting used

We don't think about how they feel
To us it's no big deal
Unfortunately, until the end of time
It will remain this way still
We will continue to kill

# So Hot

Absorbing the heat rays from the sunny sky afar
Feel as though my feet are burning from the asphalt tar
I need to hurry up and jump in my car

Instant tan
Due to my arms and hands dangling out the window
Trying to catch a cool breeze
Because the AC makes me sneeze

We beg for heat in the winter
And cold in the summer
Never satisfied
With what the good Lord provides

It's a beautiful day
The heat is okay
Stop complaining
Live out each day with a blast
One of these glorious days might be your last

# Starry Night

*I*t's a beautiful starry night
Sky lit up so bright
Nature's awesome way of providing us with light

To guide us to and fro
Wherever we need to go

Such an artistic view
Noticed by only a few
I totally understand what stargazers find appealing
The binoculars give you a true view

Up in the galaxy
So amazing to me
Another of God's mysteries

Endless stars filling the skies
Wondering what each of them symbolizes
If we knew, we'd probably be surprised
But since we don't
We'll continue to fantasize

Although thousands of miles away
An unrealistic portrait is displayed
As morning seeps through and the stars fade

Next come the glorious sun rays
To start another beautiful day
While we go on our destined ways

*Roberta Blango*

# The Thunderstorm

The rain whips across my car windows
The lightening pierces through my windshield
The thunder booms louder than the Fourth of July fireworks

Terror strikes throughout my veins
I'm about to scream
If this scene doesn't soon change

I'm behind the wheels of my SUV
Can hardly see
What's in front of me
They say this is the best place to be
I don't agree

Strong winds blowing debris all over the place
Crazy people still flying past like they are in a race
One false move and they are gone without a trace

The skies became very dark
All I could think about was
Getting somewhere safe to park

Thunderstorms, not my favorite weather
Thunder, lightning, and me, don't go well together

I would rather be in the comfort of my home
When I see sharp lightning and hear loud thunderous booms
The safest place for me is in my bedroom

# Umm...The Smells

The Smells
The Smells
The smells of so many various scents
Flowing by and through our nostrils
Bitter
Sweet
Sour
Even the fresh scent of blossomed flowers
Some smells bring joy, some sadness
Nothing beats the smell of cooking
It's the best smell of them all
Different flavors lingering out and about
Especially at cookouts
Having strangers wanting to come check it out
Then comes the fresh morning dew
To awaken you
Next, out the door
To sniff the crisp autumn air to soothe you
There are just so many pleasant smells
Even the ones that are not so well
We are so thankful and blessed
To have the sense of smell
To help us identify so many glorious things to.....
Smell
Smell
Smell
Without it
We would not be able to foretell
What comes and goes
Past our nose

We All

H

a

v

e

Self-Confidence

# I Am Me

I am me
Not the person
You're trying to make
me become

I'm not that person
I am me
Leave me
Just as I am

You might hate me
But I love me

I have no desire
To be or
Look like
Someone else

If you can't accept me
Just as I am
Then go

If you truly loved me
You wouldn't be
Trying to change me
So just let me be

I won't let you destroy
My self esteem
Because you are ashamed
To be with me

Well sweetheart
I'm setting you free
You no longer have to worry
About disappointing old me
Because I love myself
More than you

# I Love Me

*I* loved me before I met you
I love myself no less now that I've met you
I will continue to love myself now that I'm with you

If I don't love myself first, who will?
Something my mother instilled
Never let another break your free will

You say you love me
I believe you do
But there is nothing wrong
With me loving myself too

My self-esteem will never be broken by another
I have confidence in myself
Like no other

You may think I'm being conceited
But I'm not
It feels good living life like
You can't be stopped
Until you reach the top

I will let no one steal my joy
Steal my happiness
Steal the only thing I know
That makes my personality glow

I will love myself until the day I die
Even then I will cry
Because I'll have to forever
Tell myself good-bye

# I Want What I Want

I want what I want
And I'm going to get what I want
What I want may not be what you want

I'm going to work hard to get what I want
Because that's the only way I'm going to get what I want
Don't know what you'll do to get what you want

I'll let nothing stop me from getting what I want
Because I'm desperate to get what I want
Don't know how pressed you are to get what you want

I'll do whatever, whenever to get what I want
Because I'll do whatever it takes by any
means necessary to get what I want
Don't know whatever you'd do to get what you want

I'm going to go all out to get what I want
Don't care how much it costs to get what I want
Don't know if you'd go that far to get what you want

I'll sacrifice to get what I want
Because I have to have what I want
Don't know if you're willing to do that to get what you want

If you don't know by now that I don't care
What I have to do to get what I want
You must not have a desire to get what you want
But one thing is for sure
You know I'm going to get what I want
Because I want what I want
And I'll let nothing interfere with
What I Want!

# Independent Women

*A* woman was made from Adam's rib
Our bodies made to bear children
We were made to stand by our husband's side
To support and keep him strong
So women, if you think you're the head of your house
You're wrong

Women play an important role in life
You wear many hats, not just being your husband's wife

Women have come a long way from the old days
Women can now express freely what they have to say
Without getting hauled away

Women are in high-stature positions
Women own their own businesses
Women host T.V. shows
And, much much more

Women don't mind the nine to five
It keeps them vibrate and feeling alive
Somebody **Rise** up and give strong beautiful
Independent women a high five

Beautiful queens come in every shade, shape, and size
Whoever changed the rules for women was wise

# Just Me

All I have to give is just me
What you see
Is all I have to give

Don't stay if you want more
Don't waste my time
I won't waste yours

I'm not changing to be someone else
Something else
Nothing else
I'm going to stay me
True to me
Just me

Accept me for who I am
I'll accept who you are
Seems as though you like me
As I am thus far

I like myself
Don't want to be no one else
I love how the Creator created me
Just the way he wanted me to be

Don't need to perfect his work
I'm going to leave me as I am
Just me
What you see
I **Love** me

You must love yourself first
To accept another's love

Here I am
Take me
All of me
As I am
Just me

# Pretty You Are

Pretty you are
Pretty you are
Prettiness seems to take you far
Born under a golden star
Pretty one you are

Pretty you are
No problems finding a date
No problem finding your soulmate
Never having to wait
Prettiness must feel great

Pretty you are
First to be picked
Always getting treated
Pulled out chairs to be seated
Pretty ones often misunderstood
For being conceited

Pretty you are
Not many girlfriends
An abundance of men
Your choice of any guy
Until your prettiness dies

Pretty you are
Some sweet and kind
Some cold as ice
Some pretty ones having to pay the price
For having a face that looks so nice

Pretty you are
Starting out on top
Nothing in your way to be stopped
As long as you don't let your body flop

Pretty you are
Don't let it go to your head
Respect your beauty instead
Then you'll never be mistakenly misled
By envious ones wishing you were dead
Pretty ones hope you understood
What you've just read

# We've All

E
n
c
o
u
n
t
e
r
e
d

# Life Experiences

# A Day and A Life

A day and a life of experiences you go through
Some leave you happy, others leave you feeling blue
And some leave you not knowing which way to turn
Or what to do

Frustration fills your mind with cloudy thoughts
Stress and depression sit in
Leaving you not knowing where to begin

You take the good days with the bad
No need to get mad
Can't help but feeling sad
Wishing you still could depend on
Your mom and dad

Everyone, everywhere, everyday
Will stumble upon a mess of some kind
Leaving them distraught
Wanting and needing to unwind
But still peace unable to find

The life you were given
The life you're now living
Will cease on earth one day

Six feet under is where you will be
Some will be sad, others full of glee
Don't really know how they'll
Feel about me

Do you have an idea of how
Your friends and loved ones will feel
The day your life is taken
By God's will

Live your life to the fullest while you still can
If you can't seem to get it together
Ask for a little help
From our Lord and Savior's hand

# Be Careful What You Ask For

Be careful what you ask for
You just might get it

Without warning
Instantly
In the flash of an eye

It doesn't always happen
When you want it to
It happens when you least
Expect it to

Caught off guard
By its occurrence
Mentally preparing yourself
For what's to come

Instead of standing around
Looking dumb
Feeling numb
And stunned

Your wish came true
You should be happy
Instead of feeling blue
Who's fooling who

Mean what you say
Say what you mean
Or it could cause
Lots of pain

*Roberta Blango*

When you ask
Expect to get it
And deal with it
Or you're sure to
Regret it

# Been There

*I* feel as though I've walked in your shoes before
Listening to you share your story
Now I'm for sure
We've visited the same storm doors
But we survived life's wars
And the two of us aren't suffering anymore

Funny how people can walk the same path
Some so identical it makes you laugh
Because you're unaware
Until it's compared

This isn't an uncommon occurrence
It happens all the time
Just like repeated crimes

Only thing difference is maybe
The place
Time
Day
Hour
Minute
Or
Second
**Life**
So unexpected

Keeps us expressing, guessing, and stressing
Until we ask the good Lord for his blessings

# Cuz, I'm Talking 2 U

It saddens me that you've spent majority of your life behind bars
When you were blessed with a gift to fix cars

We grew up like we were sister and brother
Due to the close relationship of our mothers

We played and learned together everyday
Is what my mother used to say

We lived in the same house until it burned down to the ground

That is when our parents went their separate ways
And I was unable to see you sometimes for days

Fast money comes with a price
It is the root of all evil and comes with great sacrifice
To make you suffer and think twice

Every ordeal you've experienced is a lesson learned
But when you repeat it as though you're unconcerned
You get burned

You're getting older and you have kids to think about
It's time to start a new life's route
This time when you get out

It's never too late to change your direction
To improve your imperfections

I wish things had turned out differently for you
Please stop doing the things you used to
Take advantage of this second chance given unto you

# Don't Know Me, Don't Judge Me

You say I act wild
Try walking in my shoes for a day
Then you'll judge me another way

You can't judge a book by its cover
Come home with me and you'll discover
A child having to deal with strange men pretending to be your lover

No loving parents to protect their innocent child
Walk for miles and miles
Asking why do I have to live a life like this
Instead of being greeted daily with a hug and kiss
And parents telling me, I'm missed
Mine are crackheads and don't care that I exist

Instructed to come straight home
Because there is money to be earned
My health, no concern
So my acting wild was learned
Because of the love and attention I yearn

I have to escape this madness the best way I know how
So yes, I act out in public for attention
Can't go back to school, due to my suspension

Parents don't know and don't care
So every day I leave out of there
Going somewhere, anywhere
The way they use my body for money is unfair
They would kill me if I reported them to welfare

Foster care is just as bad
People letting me stay only to collect a check
No love, everything about the dollar bill
So yes, I act up, what do you expect

*Roberta Blango*

My life down the drain
So much pain I want to scream
Hoping someone will hear me and tell me
This horrible life I'm living is all a dream
Then I'm awakened by a whack across my brain

I'm used to the beatings
I'm so numb inside, they don't hurt anymore
I don't know how I survived
Some days I don't care if I live or die
It makes me sad, but I won't cry

I have to be strong for me
So the next time you see me acting wild
Know that I'm trying to release some inner pain

Don't judge me
If you don't know me
Try to ignore me
I'm a child scorned with no one to love me

# Forbidden Desires

A forbidden desire is invading my mind
And common sense left behind
A craving I can't seem to shake nor escape

Although I know it's wrong and not right
The temptation is incredibly hard to fight
With constant restless nights

Bad boys always the most desired
And willing to conspirer
Taking your mind, body, and soul higher
Leaving you feeling as though you're on firer

They play the game very well
Leaving you in some type of love spell
Straight from hell

They love the chase
It comes with ease and grace
Once conquered, leaves you without a trace

That forbidden fruit
In a delicious suit
Can't disappear from my brain
Leaving my soul drained

I'm entangled in his silky web
Don't want to end up in his bed
I'll choose to run instead

Must be strong
And leave him alone
Because he belongs to another
So I can't allow this to go on any further

Karma is Real
Therefore I'm going to chill
And disregard the way I feel
Over this heart throb
Before my future love gets robbed
Over a forbidden desire that I should have ignored

# Free Me

Free me
Release me
Let go of me
Make peace with me

To be free
Be able to flee
To see
What brings me glee

No restraints
No time to think
Just run go run
Before you sink

Free as birds in the sky
Wish I could fly
Way up high
Especially in July

Non-stop
Hippity hop
On the move
To some perfect spot

Don't slow me down
Not letting my feet hit the ground
Until I hear the sound
From the freedom town

Free inside and out
Is what this journey is all about
There's no joy
Than to explore
This type of feeling

That most are concealing
Instead of expressing
Their freedom and progressing
Because to be free
Is truly a blessing

# Hard Pretending to Like

*I*t takes a lot of work pretending to like someone
When you can't stand the sight of them
But you force yourself to treat them kind

It's hard eating someone's terrible meal
But it will hurt them if you tell them how you really feel
So you eat it even though inside you want to squeal

It's hard pretending you like an awful gift
You can't tell them you hate it
Therefore you take it and tell them how great it is

There are many people and things in life that we pretend to like
But on the inside we want to throw up
We are accustomed to just go with the flow
And not let folks really know

Some people can read your facial expressions
Others hide theirs well
Therefore you're unable to tell
What really dwells within
That's how well they pretend

When someone wrongs you, it hurts
Especially someone pretending to be a friend
Someone pretending they care
What can you do
Life's unfair
You must learn to become aware
Of those who pretend
Ones you know you can't trust or **depend** on

You will start to blend in just like the rest
Pretending just like the rest
Going with the flow just like the rest
Failing or passing the test just like the rest
Pretending to like is a lot of work
I'll be the first to attest

# Here But Away

My body is here
But my mind is somewhere else
Far far away
Wandering throughout the day
Paying attention to no one
Looking in their direction
But looking beyond them
Not seeing them
Not hearing them
They might as well be invisible
Because I'm here
But I'm not
Don't mean to be rude
But I can't seem to focus
I'm in a daze
Can't stop daydreaming
My mind, body, and soul
Somehow stole
And it's out of my control
An out of body experience
I guess
But nevertheless
I feel like I'm in another dimension
It's peaceful
I need to come back
To my body
To my mind
From the two worlds that intertwined
Within my brain
It's hard to explain
When you're unable to concentrate
Feeling like you're not awake
Then you get that awaited shake
Bringing you back to reality
Snap
One, two, three

# I Wanna

*I* wanna be here
I wanna be there
I wanna be everywhere

With people who care
With people who share
With people who treat me fair

When the time is right
When my smile remains bright
When it's a perfect day and night

I want it to last
I want it to be a blast
I want to live for the future
And forget about the past

Time for a new day
Time for things to go my way
Time for people to listen to
What I have to say

I wanna be free
I wanna be me
I wanna be full of glee

Wanna happy heart
Wanna fresh start
Wanna do what's smart
Wanna be together instead of apart

I wanna go
I wanna know
I wanna take it slow

Time on my side
Time to no longer hide
Time to take pride

In what I believe
In what I want to receive
In what I know I can achieve

I know it can come true
I know it depends on what I do
I know it will happen for me
And it can also happen for you

Life is what you make it
Just go for it and not waste it

# I'm Not Happy

What do you do when the love has gone away?
And you now yearn for happy days
But for unknown reasons, you continue to stay

I don't know if I'll ever find another
I may end up alone
Once he's gone

Certainly not in a rush
To get my heart crushed
From some others I don't trust

Why am I here
Is it fear?
Is it my mind that's unclear?
I just want to disappear

I'm not happy with myself anymore
This relationship is like a dreadful chore

I feel like I'm wasting my life
He's wasting his too by thinking
I'm going to one day become his wife

# I'm Trying

*I*'m like a lost puppy trying to find my way home

Trying to get through another day

Trying to keep my faith and obey

Trying to find the right words to say

Trying to do and be my best everyday

Trying to ignore friends who betray

Trying to decide if they should go or stay

Trying to figure out which bills I can afford to pay

Trying to stay away from another buffet

Trying not to be sad when a loved one passes away

Trying not to stress and learn to play

Trying not to be naïve and lead astray

Trying to discover a positive role model to lead the way

Trying to convince folks I'm blessed and will be okay

Trying not to forget to get down on my knees every night and pray

For a better day for an American to be proud they live in the

Good old

USA

# Independence Is Virtue

When you're independent
You don't have to ask anyone for a thing
You don't have to wait on anyone
You can get things done
On your own

Depending on others takes your freedom away
Have to wait on and do things their way
Even if it ruins your day
I'd rather get it done myself
Even if I have to pay

Folks take advantage of the situation
Knowing you fully depend upon them
It's not fair
If the shoe was on the other foot
They would not dare
They would start to care

Some folks are dependable
They are always ready and on time
But that's rare and hard to find
Folks are not that kind
Anymore

Times have changed
People have changed
Everyone so selfish
Think about self-first
And it's getting worst

In this day and time
You have to fend for yourself
Family and friends are the worse
A stranger would probably help you first

The key word today is
Be independent
Don't depend on anyone
If you don't
Disappointment you are sure to find
Folks going on with their plans
And leaving yours behind

# Is it My Imagination

Is it just my imagination, the way he looks at me
Like the two of us should be
He probably would try, if he was free

His eyes, I try to avoid
Don't want his relationship to be destroyed

The two of us will never be
Because I'm not free
You see

It takes two to tangle
Cheating can get people strangled

It's not worth getting hurt
So you best be on alert
The consequences over an innocent flirt

If you don't want it to escalate
Don't participate
Stop it, before it's too late

Smile and keep on going
Before you end up regretting something
You had no intention of doing

Imprison your imagination
Without hesitation
Before it causes unnecessary frustrations

# Life

*A* time in life
Life's experiences
Life trials
Can be mild
Or hostile
Depending on one's lifestyle

### Perfect Life
One wish
Hope for
Dreams of
But unfortunately
It's not heard of

### Good Life
Many have experienced
It's not uncommon
Majority of us do
Depending on what one
Has gone through
But for most it is true
That is just my point of view

### Fair Life
Another widespread category
Of those who constantly worry
Theirs tend to fluctuate
Depending on the load of their plate
One day all is well
The next, feel as though
They're going through hell

### Bad Life
Some have no control
Born with no one to console

Conditions unbearable
Started out terrible
The kind we all must pray for
Can't afford to ignore

For many, the ground is their floor
Bad lives do nothing but destroy
One's motivation
To improve their situation
It can be turned around
So the next generation
Won't have to endure the same devastation
All it takes is one
For this vicious cycle
To come undone
And a new one begun

# Life is What You Make It

$S$uch a broad statement
But a true statement
Life will be what you make it

You have the power to do and be
Whatever you want to be
You have control of your destiny

Put your mind to it and do it
And pray that it will come to be
You'll be surprised by the outcome of
Your dreams and goals
Becoming a reality

Life can and will be a challenge in many areas
You'll have to be strong
Don't worry about situations when they go wrong

Pick up the pieces and keep on going
No one is aware of the unknowing
We learn from our mistakes and continue growing

Take the good with the bad
Be the best at the part you have been given
To play in this world
Doesn't matter if you're a boy or a girl

In life there will be happy days
There will be sad days
There will be days that make you
Fall to your knees and give praise
Start living life like there's no tomorrow
And you will be amazed

You can either live it, quit it, or fake it
But the fact remains,
Life will only be what you make it

# Life's Twists

Our lives are like winding roads
Full of twists and turns
Lots of lessons to learn

Some happy some sad
Some good some bad
Some too embarrassing to add

We have to force ourselves to keep going
Life doesn't stop
When something causes our jaws to drop
Or a decision we've made has flopped

Your head steaming
You feel like screaming
Wished you were dreaming

Reality slaps you in the face
Too late to erase
Too late to correct
Too late to uncheck
What we've wrecked

You cry
Want to die
Ask yourself
Over and over
Why

It's just another trial
To add to our pile
In the end
The lessons we learn
Are all worthwhile

# Life's Twists & Turns

*L*ife
Can be good
Can be bad
Some wish they never had
It!

Some say life
Is what you make it
Sometimes that's true
Sometimes it depends
On your circumstances

Everyone doesn't have
A good life experience
Some folks are born
In a destructive situation

Leaving life unappealing
Unable to deal
With what they went through
You wouldn't understand
Unless it happened to you

Some born with a silver spoon
Were given the moon
Spoiled brats
Grow up and don't know how to act

That's life
Full of twists and turns
Some worked hard
To get to the top
Others lost the urge
And simply stopped

Everyone isn't born with that itch
To get rich

People get off track
For numerous life's reasons
Some pop back
Others, motivation they lack

Life is always worth living
Although some things are unforgiving
But you must try
Until the day you die

Love yourself
Even if nobody else does
No one can love your life
Better than you!

# Mind Games

Mind games of the worst kind
Mixed signals
Unable to define
A truthful sign

People will say and do anything
To achieve their objective
Use you in the worst way
You become their prey

Destroying
Whoever
Whenever
Whatever
It takes to accomplish their goal
Releasing their true inner soul
So very cold

Don't even realize what hit you
Until it's too late
Like you're daydreaming
Not fully awake
But it's real, not fake
A weak mind is all it takes

To become a victim
Of such a predator
Doesn't take much
You have been singled out
For the hunt
They will use every stunt
And they have a bunch

You're going to have to
Rescue your mind
Take back control
Break the manipulative hold
And roll

Regain your freedom
Your mind, body, and soul
It won't be easy
But well worth pleasing
To end the grasp
That's been squeezing
The life out of you
Become renewed
Chances of most escaping
Are few
So lucky are you

# Missing That Spark

I feel as though something is missing
No sparks flying
No hugs and kissing

The desire evades me
I know this isn't the way true love is supposed to be
Therefore it can't possibly be he
That's right for me

I want to feel electrified
Just from his touch
Want to light up as soon as I see his face
And miss him greatly when he's not in my space

True love is so hard to find
Folks today are good at playing with your mind
Can't trust a soul
Because people are so cold
It's starting to get very old

I pray one day
The Lord will send the right one my way
Until then……
I rather be alone
Safely in my cocoon
Hopefully he'll cross my path soon

# Never Thought

Never thought life would change like this
The everlasting bliss I missed
No knight in shining armor to kiss

Everything in life happens for a reason
Guess it's just not my season
But I'll keep the faith and believing

A necessary break I'll take
Until my inner soul awakes
To someone hopefully real and not fake

Times have definitely changed
And this new dating scene is quite strange
The women have to ask for a guy's name
What a frightening thing

Never thought I'd be in this situation
On my own with life's complications

Nevertheless, if this is how it's meant to be
I'll let it be
Alone and free
With just me
It's better than being stuck in misery

# No Feelings Left

There's an empty hole in my heart
And there's no feeling left
I'm tired trying to convince myself

I have no more tears to shed
No more love to spread
Want no more lies cluttering my head

I'm looking forward to a better day
Happy to get away
It would be dumb to stay

It's the right thing to do
After all I've been through

I didn't think I had the strength to leave
The devil will make you naïve
But the Lord will intervene and help you believe

Wrong or right
These feelings didn't vanish overnight
They've developed over the years and
Now they've come to light

I have to start living for me
Despite who may disagree

This is my life and I'm going to change it around
Tired of wearing a frown
I'm going to stand firm and not back down

I'm out the door
Because love doesn't live in my heart anymore
I'm free and no longer feel as though I'm a prisoner of war

# No Love For Me

Mr. Right doesn't exist
He seems to be a mystery

How have I experienced so many
No love found in any

Think I was doomed from the start
With a stone-cold heart

Unbreakable
Solid as a rock
As the time clock
Tick tock

It's a very sad situation
Not finding true relations

Just going with the flow
Isn't the way to go

Think I missed that love train
It has never been a section of my brain
With sounds insane

I thought love was a natural act
For some it's a fact
But for people like me
Finding true love
Is like finding a thousand-year-old artifact

# Our Actions

Everything we do in life depends on our actions
How we react
If we react
Why we react
When we react
All depend on the outcome of our actions

It could impact our life
Our family's life
Our work life
Our friend's life
A stranger's life
Anyone can be affected by our actions

That's why it's so important
To think before we react
A simple word of advice
Could get you back on track
And that's a fact

We need to open up more
Don't be afraid to ask for
Help from family, friends, or
The neighbor next door

We can all control our actions
It is all in our minds
We just need help to unwind
And find
That place deep within that we've left behind
When we were confused and blind

Turn that negative action
Into a positive action
And we will get a rejuvenating reaction
To our satisfaction

# Rich, but Sad

*I* have it all
Anything I want
At my fingertips
But yet,
Still not satisfied
Still not happy
Still missing something
That money can't buy
It will consume me
Until the day I die
Is it...**Love** and **Happiness**?
That my heart desires
Is that what I need?
To take me higher
To change this inner pain
That's driving me insane
Is all this money to blame?
For the outcome of this lonely person
I became
Money, the number one thing
Everyone craves
But you can't take it to your grave
Although it's good to have
But what good is it
If you can't buy
What's going to put a smile upon my face
Happiness can't be replaced
Doesn't matter how rich a person may be
Happiness remains free
And it's the only thing
That's going to change **Me**!

# So Drained

My body is so drained
So is my brain
Amongst other things

So tired I can hardly
Keep my eyes open
Keep my head lifted
Keep my body from slouching

Can't think straight
Can't participate
Can someone relate?

One of these days
Constantly in a daze
Want to try and get myself together
But this fatigue won't leave
It stays

So much caffeine
Trying to jumpstart my brain
Energy still in the distance
Nowhere to be seen

I need to put pep in my step
Maybe a Red Bull would help

Getting the proper rest
Is the remedy that works best
It will alleviate unnecessary stress

So sleep, sleep, sleep
Don't open your eyes until
Your alarm clock beeps

So whatever it takes to help you
Whether it's a
Strong soda
Coffee or tea
Sleep is what works for me

# So Sick Of

So sick of people constantly complaining

So sick of this corrupt economy

So sick of injustice

So sick of people suffering

So sick of jealousy

So sick of people's backstabbing ways

So sick of procrastination

So sick of blasphemy

So sick of the fake and pretend

So sick of wars overseas

So sick of overcrowded roadways

So sick of extremely loud noise

So sick of immature adults acting like kids

So sick of paying bills

So sick of people who kill

*Roberta Blango*

So sick of not fulfilling my dreams

So sick of being stressed

So sick of not getting the proper rest

So sick of dealing with the day to day
State of affairs to survive to stay alive

# Tears

Tears streaming down your face
For many reasons
Some sad ones
Some joyful ones
Some painful ones
Some pleasurable ones
Falling, falling
Caused by uncontrollable emotions
You wipe them away
Indicating you're okay
But your insides are still churning
From the emotional outbreak
Leaving your face looking like a lake
Tears are a part of human nature
Doesn't matter if you're female or male
When your eyes start to wail
It's out of your control
Tears, a form of silent communication
Alerting that something's right or wrong
Just from the display of tears on your face
Let them flow
Let them show
Let them go.. go.. go..
And if someone sees you shedding them
So… so…so…

# That Mean Green Dollar Bill

That dollar bill can be good
Or it can be bad
It makes some folks miserable and sad
And wish they never had

It's the root of all evil
But we all need it to survive
To stay alive

People do all sorts of things to get that dollar bill
Some steal, lie, and kill
Over that mean green dollar bill

It can break up the closest friends
Bring years of marriage to an abrupt end
Yet it is something we all crave
Quite hard to comprehend
This money which we love to spend

Life of luxury
Comfortable
Can't complain
Yet drives some folks insane

Some say the richest
Are the saddest
Some say they are
The gladdest
Others say
The maddest

What do you think?
About that mean green dollar bill

How would it make you feel?
Would you lose your mind?
OR
Would it be no big deal?
And you'd continue to stay chilled

# Wasted The Best of Me

*I*t's an indescribable feeling
When most of your life you've been concealing
Something that prevents your heart from healing
Now at an age that's a bit too late for revealing

A sacrifice for one of the loves of my life
Still kills me to know that I could have been
some other guy's loving wife
A decision I now regret
If only I had my current mindset

They say in life we live and we learn
Even sometimes getting burned
Which leave the fragile heart scorned
And a woman's life transformed

Leaving her mind, body, and soul just a little tougher
Ensuring he next life experience will be smoother
Although there is no guarantee
How the next outcome will be

Approaching the next situation a lot wiser
Able to decipher
Those undercover liars

Hoping to experience tranquility
With a newfound stability
Don't know if a soulmate exists for me
But now at this age what will be will be
Even if it ends up with just being lonely old me

I'd rather be happy and alone
Then in a loveless relationship doomed
I'm at the halfway point
Where I have a clearer viewpoint

Know exactly what I want
Not saying he must be perfect
But I'm going to definitely make sure
Every I is dotted and every T is crossed
Or he will be immediately tossed!!

# Your Heart Doesn't Lie

Listen closely to your heart
It warns you from the start
We ignore it, which isn't smart

Your emotions can trick your mind
Saneness unable to find
Love is blind

You had a gnawing feeling deep within
But you continued to ignore it again and again
Lust always wins

Love or lust
You must make a choice
Listen to your inner voice

To guide you down the right path
You're going to either cry or laugh
Depending on the aftermath

Happiness should be your ultimate goal
If true love isn't seeping from your soul
You're sure to regret the wrong decision
Until you're gray and old

Your heart doesn't lie
So when you think you've met the apple of your eye
But your heart is telling you to keep walking by
Don't ask why

The unknowing is sometimes best
Than taking a guess
On it being a success or a hot mess

# Your Song, My Life

*I*s my life like a song?
Is the song a reflection of my life?
Depends on who's telling the story
What version
When in my life
Who in my life
Where in my life
Why are you interested in my life?

What harmony describes my life?
Oldie but Goodies
R&B
The Blues
Pop
Country
Rock & Roll
Jazz
Guess it depends on the mood, if I was happy, sad, or mad

The future, present, or past
Is what you must first ask
Got to get the song right
If you want me to give you the green light
The approval of my life's story
Take your time there's no hurry

Can't wait to hear the words escape your mouth
Will I cry or will I laugh
Will I start to reminisce about what I've missed?
Will I be able to endure the impact?
Of your soulful track
I promise not to overreact

*Roberta Blango*

Soothing and smooth is how your melody flows
Not too fast or too slow
Your sweet angelic voice singing my life's story
So glad I chose you, I'm no longer worried

No one could have described my life any better
I couldn't have told it better myself
You expressed every aspect of my life
And now your song and my life are on the charts as number one
Job well done!

We've All

F

e

l

t

Angry

# Cold Cold World

This world can be so very cold
Cold to the young
Cold to the old
Cold to anyone that's not bold

Not bold enough to bully back
Not bold enough to tell them take a hike
Not bold enough to fight back
Due to the monstrous way they act

Being so cruel
Always wanting to rule
The weak
By the harsh way they speak

Someone may have done the same to them
So they want to take their revenge out on you
Which is unfair to you
But what are you to do

Many take their suppressed anger out on the wrong people
The innocent bystander
Because they are too afraid to face their real opponent

The one who destroyed their mind
Leaving behind
A lost person
A distraught being
With a heart cold as ice
Incapable of being nice

It tends to escalate as they get older
Colder and colder
More vicious
A viciousness that lands them in jail
All because of some adult female or male
Doing harm to them as a child and they were too afraid to tell

# Hate Crimes

Hate, a mighty strong word
To hate your fellow
Brothers and sisters
No matter gender or race
Is a disgrace

The Lord made us all as one
To love and get along with one another
Not to kill each other

It's a shame
Killing and beating folks
Then say the color of skin,
Religion, sexual orientation
Is the blame

Who gave them the authority to judge
Those types of people have extreme hate deep within
They have no consciousness of this great sin
Because they are quick to tell you
Given the chance, they'd do it again

A cold heart
From the start
Taught at an early age
Over years turned to rage

We are all born to love
Straight from the Lord up above
Then the devil sticks his hand in
And interrupts and people
End up corrupt

Time for change is well overdue
The pain and suffering hate crimes put families through
A very cowardly act
The way they attack

Most victims are unaware
Until it's too late to escape
Damage done
Then the perpetrators on the run
Leaving the world stunned

To hate is enough
But to hate and commit crimes
Because you hate
Is a lethal combination
That's sure to cause devastation
To our loving nation

# You Say You Don't Remember Me

You say you don't remember me
You lie, you lie, I saw it in your eyes
That little twinkle and how your face wrinkled

You didn't even take a minute to think
How we'd first linked
You were gone in a blink

You may have forgotten my name
But my face is still the same
You're just lame

Yes, we ended on a bitter note
But sixteen years has gone bye
And you still feel the need to lie
WHY!

Let the past be the past
You shouldn't let your bitterness last
Forgiveness is all I ask

I went on with my life
And you went on with yours
I see you now have a beautiful wife

Pretending you didn't know me hurt
It made me feel less than dirt
Two wrongs don't make a right
You got your sweet revenge back tonight

Are we even
Are you done grieving
If not, I'm done begging and
I'm leaving

I can't change the way you feel about me
I can't force you to talk to me
I can't make you forgive me
I can't force you to listen to me
But what I can't comprehend most is
You acting like you don't remember me!

# Who'd Ever Thought

Who'd ever thought there would be days like this?
Your life spun out in a twist
Letting folks get you pissed
Telling them what they can kiss

Who'd ever thought you'd let them get under your skin
Letting them win
Instead of displaying a grin
Above your chin

Who'd ever thought you'd let them see you sweat
In and out of debt
Lost another bet
No time to get upset

Who'd ever thought you wouldn't obey
Not listening to a word they say
Thinking your callous actions are okay
Because you didn't get your way

Who'd ever thought you'd let life get you down
Constantly wearing a frown
Wishing you were six feet under ground
Never to be found

You never thought going to church would turn your life around
Have you singing a different tune
Can't always resolve issues on your own
Sometimes you can't do it alone

Who'd ever thought they'd see that beautiful smile upon your face
Saved by God's loving grace
You never thought there would be a day
when all your troubles got erased
By you getting down on your knees to pray
And witnessing Him making them all disappear without a trace

Who'd ever thought it would happen to me
And it can also happen to you too
Now that you know what to do

We've All

F

e

l

t

Hopelessness

# Broken Wing

*L*ife has destroyed one wing
And is beating down on the good one
Too much to handle, I'm almost done
Flying with one wing is no fun

Broken inside and out
Can't win for losing
Luck just not on my side
This is no longer amusing

Need to improve the paths I'm choosing
Seems so confusing
Need to embark on a new endeavor
If I plan to change my life forever

Not going to be easy
Going to take some time
I'm willing to take a chance
To regain my happy dance

Want to smile again
Want to laugh again
Want to live again
Without stress and pain

I've learned life is no bed of roses
There will be good and bad times ahead
But you can't let it take over and
Keep you buried down
Wearing a depressing frown

You have to pray about it and
Face it full force with all the strength
You have in your body instead

# I'm Broken

Broken
From
Birth
Till
Whenever

Life started out rough
Left in a dumpster like trash
Because my mom had no cash
That in itself messes with my brain
Makes me want to scream
Forget about self-esteem
That I lack
Because my mother smoked crack
Leaving me a newborn addict
My life you can predict
No love ever received
Ever since I was conceived
Can you believe?
How could the one that's supposed
To love you be the most deceitful
Hearts unmendable
Actions unpredictable
Life miserable
Don't understand the meaning of love
Never experienced love
Never received or given love
I'm broken inside and out
My entire life without
A person to care about
**ME!**
So you see
This is how you turn out
When both parents are
Absentees!

# It's Hard

*I*t's hard to avoid your handsome face
But your bad attitude makes it easy to erase
Disappearing without a trace

It's hard to forget the gentleness of your touch
But when you drink too much and start to hit
It makes me want to split

It's hard for me to forget the good times
I wished they outweighed the bad
But they don't and it makes me sad

It's hard for me not to think of your sweet lips
That's until you flipped
Leaving my tooth chipped

It's hard not to reminisce about our special rendezvous
But the way you started treating me
Made it easy for me to fall out of love with you

It's hard to forget how I thought you completed me
Until I opened up my love-blinded eyes and can plainly see
That we were **Never** meant to be

It's no longer hard for me to forget about you
It was love and hate all wrapped up in one
And what's done is done
The past can't be undone
But by leaving you
I now realize
I've won

# No Hope Left

My heart no longer in my chest
It now lies at the bottom of my feet

I can't control this urge to split
To give up and quit

So unhappy so sad
It's gotten that bad

We need to go our separate ways
That's the only thought I have these days

The disrespect has gone too far
And it's leaving an ugly scar

I must muster up the strength to leave
So I can be free and breathe

**Again**

With or without a man

# Suicide Is Never The Answer

$I$ get it
Life can be rough at times
Take you through some of the toughest days
Trials you think are unbearable
And extremely terrible
But through God
They are repairable
Don't be so quick to react
To the devil's attack
Be patient
And allow God to get you
Back on track
Suicide
Causes such devastation
You destroy the Lord's creation
You
A gift so special
Each year it's celebrated
With love affiliated
Taking your life is
Never the answer
Never the way to resolve it
Never the way out of
Whatever the situation or
Circumstance is about
It may seem bleak
Making you weak
Not wanting to speak
But this is the perfect time
To seek
The Lord
He will go over and beyond
Creating a special bond
Instantly erasing all the pain

And low self esteem
Rejuvenating your brain
He will pull you out of that black hole
Take control
And replenish your soul
Many don't believe until they receive
I'd prefer you give Him a try
Than to die

# What About Me

It gets hard trying to stay strong all the time
Trying to keep a smile on my face
To keep from crying
I'm no different from the next
My life is just as complex
I get weak
And want to weep
Need someone to wipe my tears
Want to share my pain
Need someone to keep me sane
Self-esteem dwindling down
Can't seem to erase this frown
My life needs to turn around
Need someone to lift me up
Tell me everything going to be alright
I'm going to take a deep breath
And try to get myself together
It must get better
Better for me
Better for you
Better for whatever you're going
Through!

# What Did I Do or Didn't Do

*I*'m encountering some of the darkest days
Nothing seems to be going my way
I often wonder.......
Is it something I did?
Is it something I said?
That was inappropriate
Now I'm being punished
Although I can't remember
Saying or doing anything to cause
This catastrophe in my life
When I take three steps forward
I fall five steps backwards
When things are looking good
Bad comes creeping around the corner
Pushing and forcing me down on my knees
Down to the ground, dignity nowhere to be found
Depression sets in, stress circling my brain
Watching everyone else around me doing good
Like I should, like I could, like I would
If bad luck would stop knocking down my door
There must be something better in store
For me, my life
All this bad luck
I can't seem to duck
Therefore, I'm feeling stuck
Rooted underground
No one to hear my cry
My struggles
My defeat
Please someone come rescue me
I need help, I'm asking for help

To see a better day
When things start going my way
And my life is back on track and okay
I'll be the first one to say
Thank You Lord for this day
Without delay

We've All

F
e
l
t

Proud

# Beauty

Nothing's like beautiful sceneries that makes
your eyeballs stare in amazement

Makes your jaw drop in awe

Makes your imagination go wild

Makes you want to express your feelings in front of a large crowd

Makes your thoughts wonder, how

And your mouth says, Wow!

Sends chills up your spine

Makes you almost lose your mind

A unique vision

A masterpiece of perfection

Of an artist's reflection

A gift like no other

Inherited from his/her father or mother

Genius

One's opinion

Of such exquisite sights

**Beauty**

It's what

Everyone likes

# Proud Daddy

My baby will be here in nine months
Don't care what the sex, girl or boy
Because whatever the sex
It's going to bring my life
An abundance of joy

I'm going to be the best dad I can be
To this precious child who's a part of me
To love and cherish to the third degree
Yes, that's me, **Proud Daddy** to be

Growing inside its moms belly to survive
Until the joyous day he/she arrives
Healthy and alive

I'm going to be right there to hear his/her first cry
To see him/her open their eyes
And remember and cherish that moment until the day I die
Because we all know how time flies

Sweet, sweet, child of mine
Look how the smile on your dad's face shines
Yes, **Proud Daddy**, on cloud ninety-nine

So soft and cuddly with that newborn smell
Can't wait to get on my cell
And tell everyone
My bundle of joy has exited its mother's shell
And is doing well

**Proud Daddy** shedding some tears
And welcomed a new life into this world
To love and protect for the remainder of his years

Yes, it's a **Boy**!

# Vain U R Not

**B**eautiful and **Breathtaking**
But still not vain
Your beauty doesn't mean a thing
To you, you're the same
Your personality defies the stereotyped ones
We're used to seeing

Arrogance doesn't flow through your veins
You don't let your beauty inflate your brain
Acting snobby and insane
Like the other beauty queens

You're sweet, innocent, and shy
Please remain that way till you die
Your beauty will take you far
Possibly becoming a movie star
Just don't forget where you came from
And who you are

You get plenty of attention
Everywhere you go
Therefore, you know
You're hot
And have your pick
That gorgeous smile always does the trick

You were blessed with good looks
Guys getting infatuated and hooked
Brains and beauty too
Lucky you

True beauty comes from within
And you display it inside and out
You will always stand out in a crowd
The Lord made you flawlessly beautiful
So be proud

We All

H

a

v

e

Dreams & Talents

# A Dream

*A* dream is dead if you don't make it come alive
Make it come to be
Make it a reality

Procrastination will hold you back
Work hard, don't let anything or anyone throw you off track
Dreams do come true and that's a fact

A dream is what you make it
**Fantasy** or **Reality**
You choose
You're either going to win or lose

I'd rather give it a try
Then let it die
Flushing it down the drain
Twenty years later asking yourself why

Dream big
Dream small
Just give it your all
Even if you fall

It's never too late to fulfill a dream
Although that's how it may seem
But erase that negativity from your brain

I don't want to see dreams go to waste
Don't want them to diminish
Want soulful dreams to replenish
Then let the good Lord finish

*Roberta Blango*

What He has installed
For us all
Ever since He birthed us and our names were called

Keep your dreams alive
And you're sure to one day thrive

# Ancient Beauty

*A* silent night it is
Quiet as a mouse
In this old ancient house
Silent, yes it is

Old, but can't hear squeaks in the floor
Or had I ignored
Signs that it's been restored
The floors aren't old anymore

Furniture still the same
Beautiful antique frames
To throw it away would be a shame
Priceless if only for the brand name

Built solid
Made to last
For generations to pass
Still standing but on less grass
Due to built-up trash

Some complain
Saying it's the ugliest they've ever seen
Just a little stained
Nothing that can't be cleaned

All it needs is some TLC
Clear up the weeds and dust
Plant some trees remove the leaves
Bring it back to life
Making it the phenomenal house it used to be

This ancient beauty still has lots of wearing
And tearing to go
Don't critique it by what you see

Believe me
With the right imagination and decoration
This old house will one day be
The subject of many conversations
Due to its well-preserved historic foundation

# Don't Give Up

*D*on't give up when things aren't going as you've planned
Get back up again and again
Persistence will help you to obtain, and not
let negativity enter your brain

Disappointment can drive some people crazy, then
They give up and get lazy

You have to fight for your dream
Don't give up and scream
Pump fuel back into your veins to uplift your self-esteem
RECLAIM YOUR DREAM!

Don't expect everyone to have your back
You'll be surprised by how some will react
The hurt will leave an impact

Keep on doing what you're doing
Embrace the unknowing
Don't let them interfere with where you're going

Some folks don't like to see others achieve
It's hard to conceive,
The feedback you expect, but never receive

Ones you thought were close
Will disappoint you the most

You must wear thick skin
From beginning to end
I highly recommend

The road to success will be a bumpy ride
You're not given an instructor's guide
You enter into it with your eyes opened wide
People may or may not stand by your side

But when you're blessed with a gift, don't let it go to waste
Try to succeed at your own pace
When you're done, know that you've done your best, and
Put a rewarding smile upon your face

# Got That Itch

Got that itch
To get rich
And I can
With the right pitch

When determined
Nothing can hinder
Your life's agenda

Got to work hard
And give it your all
So you'll be ready
When success calls

Reach far
Let them know
Who you are
Born to be a star

Keep the desire
To go higher and higher
It's what's required

To reach the top
Don't ever stop
Use your gifts wisely
And you're sure to rise

You'll achieve
If you believe
In yourself

*Roberta Blango*

Your itch is unique
Only for you to critique
For better or worst
Dive into your dream
Headfirst

# Keep Your Dream Alive

Some people's dreams come true right away
Others may come another year, month, or day
But don't give up, it's on its way

May take a little longer than the next
Yours may be more complex
Stay with it and it'll be all you expect
And more

Keep doing your part
Whatever the Lord's placed in your heart
From the very start

There may be a challenge or two
That may come against you
But don't let that consume your view
Continue to follow through

It will benefit you in the end
You won't be able to comprehend
How your life will transcend
Everyone wanting to be your best friend

Work hard to fulfill your dreams
As hard as it may seem
That's what it sometimes takes
To claim your fame

# Poets

There are exceptional poets all over the world
Sharing their talents and expressing how they feel
Some appreciate it, to others it's no big deal

Its rhythmic flow
Lifts your spirit when you're feeling low
Just take your time and read the verses slow

It's amazing how words are compiled
To create a beautiful melody
Coming together like ingredients in a recipe

It's like music to your ears
Leaves impressions that lasts for years
Some make you laugh, others bring on tears
Keep you a good poetry book near

It's a magical creation
Can improve your relation
With one dictation
On any occasion

Poems don't discriminate
They touch every avenue
There's one sure to relate to you

Every poet has his or her own unique style
Guaranteed to produce a smile
And it's always worthwhile

Read a poem to relax your mind
Inner peace you'll find
Leaving your stress and worrying behind

# The Limelight

*D*on't think I'm ready for the limelight
Flashing cameras blinding my sight
Every day and night

Paparazzi in my face
Scoping out my place
Making up stories that's a disgrace

Want to be heard, but not seen
Want to express myself without using my name
Want to live out my dream

Taking longer than expected
My career will not be neglected
I treasure the gift the Lord gave me and respect it

It takes money to succeed
At your own speed
And lots of documents to read

One wrong move could end your career
Every person you meet is not honest and sincere
Although that's the way they may appear

The Lord will make it happen when it's my time to shine
Until then, I'll be just fine

We All

H

a

v

e

Regrets

# Addiction

He said he loves me, but he loves his addiction more
This man whom I once adored
Is on his way out the door
Because this addiction, I can no longer ignore

It's a problem and he needs help
That's the first step
Nothing is going to change until
He recognizes the problem
And ask for help to solve them

An addiction can turn your life upside down
Stop others from coming around
Addictions are hard to hide in a small town

You lie and lie
Making your loved ones cry
So afraid one day you're going to die
Because you're not willing to try
To tell this addiction good-bye

It controls your mind
Forcing you to think it's the only way to unwind
Making you treat others unkind
This addiction is getting worse and that's
Not a good sign

It's going to be hard, but
You must let it go
It destroys your body and
It's starting to show
Thought I should let you know

Do the right thing
And get into swing
So you'll have total control of the terrible things
Addiction brings

# Carelessly Involved

Reckless love is
Dangerous love
Which causes
Chaotic love
The kind that smart people
Don't become a part of

Always fun in the beginning
Until it comes time for the ending
Then you find out one was only pretending
That's when things start quickly descending
Upset over all the wasted time they've been spending
Left with a heart that needs mending

Outcome can be devastating
Even frustrating
Hearts deceived
Over the lies one believed

It takes two to tango
Usually starts with a simple hello
And there you go
A throw
From Cupid's arrow
The rest you know

You are aware of your affair
You made the choice to go there

All your common sense up in the air
You no longer care
Even though your mind is screaming beware
Of the unforeseen nightmare

Although it feels right
You know it's wrong
And you should leave the person alone
Instead you tell yourself
We're both grown
And continue to condone
A relationship with a person
That's not your own

Karma comes back
To attack
Your selfish act
And that's a fact

# Cover Up

What a hell of a life
Living a lie
Living like nothing's wrong
Just going along
With this crap
I need a slap
A woman's intuition is never wrong
There's a the time when you have to be strong

Sad in it
Will be sad without it
But I'm no longer going to ignore it
I need peace inside my head
To stop the constant tears I shed

Deep within I know I'm being misled
By his inner secret
A secret he needs to express
Thinking no one will ever guess

I feel like a fool
For sticking around so long
My insides clinch at
The thought of his touch
This is starting to be too much

For me to handle
The anger is starting to escape
I can no longer control it
Think I don't know
It easily shows

*Roberta Blango*

Every time one's near
In front or rear
I feel the tension in the atmosphere

Keep telling myself
My self-esteem is low
You know you should go

I may be home alone for a while
But I can no longer fake this lifestyle
I can't be his crutch
I love my life too much

# How Could You!

How could you dispose of your newborn baby like trash
It sickens me to ask
There are so many couples out here who would have paid you cash
People need to take time and think before reacting so fast

My heart sunk into my chest
Words I could not express
When I saw the article of a precious helpless baby
Thrown in the trash as though he/she was worthless

My eyes full of tears
For this child who wasn't given an opportunity,
to live out the years
That the Lord had planned for this sweet dear

It blows my mind
When I see this type of destructive behavior
Of precious gifts provided by our Lord and Savior

This innocent baby didn't ask to be here
Didn't volunteer
Didn't want to interfere
Yet you gave birth and then took it upon yourself,
to make he/she disappear
How can you live with yourself after committing such a heinous act
year after year?

You can't tell me you had no other choice
If only you had listened to your inner voice
The voice inside your head
Trying to stop you
Trying to reason with you
Trying to tell you
What if your mother had done the same to
YOU!

*Roberta Blango*

Precious little one
Protected by your guardian angel
Protecting you from the smelly trash and all
Caught and took you up to heaven   .
Before your little body even touched down
Now you're up in heaven with God
In your pretty white gown
You're in a better place
Full of grace
In God's loving embrace!

# I was Wrong

*I* admit, I was wrong
I should have never left you
You were and still are everything to me
The grass isn't always greener on the other side
I'm human, I made a humongous mistake
I admit it with open arms
Please take me back
My senses then, I lacked
I realize I'm nothing without you in my life
You're my all and all
I want you to be my better half
I want to make you laugh
The way you used to
Before I hurt you
I promise from the depths of my heart and soul
I will never ever deceive you, or
Cause that kind of pain again
I'm down on my hands and knees
Begging you please
Give me one more chance
To prove my love for you is real
To endure the test of time
Place your hands in mine
I pray forgiveness you'll find
Joy in your life is all I want to bring
As I place on your finger this engagement ring
Please call all your family and friends, and
Inform them, our wedding is back on schedule for this **Spring!**

# She's Not You

*I* find myself reminiscing about you more and more
Although I'm with someone new

I love her, but something is off
She doesn't make me feel like you used to

I miss the little things
That I took for granted

Wished I had them back
Sometimes, wished I had you back,
In fact

But I know that's impossible
We have separate lives
I still miss the way you squint your eyes
When you got upset

Fond memories of you and me
Won't depart from my mind
Can't seem to leave them behind

Never should have taken her to our favorite spot
Now can't erase the thoughts
Of you and me

It's not fair to my new woman
So I must stop
But
I will cherish our memories forever
I must store them away
Because
I'm married to her now
And not to you

# Temptation

As a human being
We are all tempted
Tempted to do good
Tempted to do bad
Temptation can ruin life's relations

You must be careful
And exert self-control
Nothing's worth losing your soul

Stick to the golden rules
And you'll never lose
Or have to worry about the decisions you choose
There'll be nothing to defuse

Acting on temptation
Can destroy
Take your joy
Make life not worth living anymore

It's more likely to be tempted
To do bad than good
It's sad but true
That's just my point of view
Guess it depends on
Who you're talking to

Temptation
A form of eye candy
Teasing
Deceiving
Leaving folks grieving

Temptation
Takes your breath away

With no words left to say
Know it's wrong, but your mind tells you, it's okay
Just don't forget to ask for forgiveness and pray

Temptation
Such a strong powerful word
Makes one shiver when heard
Automatically assuming doing wrong
All day long
To tempt
Can lead to contempt
So it's better to avoid it
And split

If you want to be happy
Never allow temptation to enter your mind
And forever peace you'll find

# What Goes Around Comes Around

Bad things you do in life
Come back to haunt you in the worst way
Got away with it then
But suffering for it today
Karma doesn't play

Young and dumb
Carefree
Reckless
Heartless
Stress free
Too blind to see
That you don't get away with
Treating people crappy
Without getting a dose of life's reality

You learn too late
That you should take advantage of good things
When they are presented
Or you'll definitely end up resenting
Start reminiscing about
What could have been
Back then
When
You were still a ten

They say in life
You have to take the good
With the bad
Even when you're upset and sad
Or raving mad
It won't help the problem
It just adds

You try and try
You ask yourself WHY and WHEN
This **Karma** is going to end
It happened way back then
Promising yourself
Never to do it again
Then getting down on your knees
Praying and asking God to forgive you
For all the hurt and pain you've caused
AMEN!!

# Words Hurt

*H*urtful words can last a lifetime
They can inflict the deepest pain
Forever inside your brain
People **Stop** being so mean

The worst is when it comes from
Those you love the most
Their words can rip you apart
Breaking your heart

You must be careful of the words you choose
Hurtful words can come back to haunt you one day
From a child's ego bruised and left confused
Because a parent will be the last one excused

Say what you mean
And mean what you say
But do it with tact
Without ruining someone's day

Think of other's feelings
Think of how you'd want to be treated
Turn this negativity around
So it will not be repeated
Compliment instead!

We All

N

e

e

d

Alone Time

# Soaring

*W*ish I could disappear in the sky
Up so very high
With beautiful wings to fly

Across the oceans and the seas
Inhaling the fresh cool breeze
Up higher than the tallest trees

Flying with the birds
Along with their flocks
Around the clock

So free
So happy
To be alive
Happy to be me

Clear pretty blue skies
Soaring through the clouds
For miles and miles

No scheduled destination
No complications
Want to keep going
And enjoy what I'm doing

Soaring up above
Like the sweet innocent doves
Filled with love

Soaring..........

Soaring.......

Soaring......

# Two is Company, Three is a Crowd

Two is company, three is a crowd
Adding more people, it will start to get loud

Two is company, three is a crowd
Things will get a little wild

Two is company, three is a crowd
That's why only two are allowed

Two is company, three is a crowd
It's ok if you're a child

Two is company, three is a crowd
Won't make your mate proud

Two is company, three is a crowd
Gets distorted when compiled

Two is company, three is a crowd
Three or more driving you crazy, is putting it mild

Two is company, three is a crowd
Adding more is just not my style

Just us two
Don't need the crew
To do what we want to do

We've All

B

e

e

n

In Love

# Baby I Love You

I love the way you look into my eyes
I love your smell
I love how you walk
Love your voice
Love when you call me *baby*
It really makes my day
Your romantic kisses
Love the way you love me back
In all that you do
Showing me you care
Our souls melted into one
Never to come undone
Mates for life
Promise
Never to break your heart
My love so strong
Forbids me to do wrong
You're on my mind all day and night long
I'm yours signed, sealed, and delivered
You stamped my heart
With your love
And I stamped yours in return
All doubts adjourned
I'm going to be good to you **Baby**
You're a dream come true

# Bitter Sweet Love

*I* love him, I love him not
I love when we hang out at our favorite spot
I love him not, when he's showing off acting like some big-shot

I love when he treats me like I'm the center of his universe
But I hate when his evil side emerges

I love his sweet kisses and gentle touch
But I hate when he drinks too much

I love the way he looks into my eyes
But I hate his deceitful lies

I love when he whispers sweet nothings in my ear
But sometimes his actions are unclear
And it makes me wonder if he's really sincere

I love when we cuddle and snuggle up close
But his bad habits are gross

I love his beautiful smile
But I hate his ghetto style
I'm so confused, I'm starting to wonder
If it's all worthwhile

Our relationship is bitter and sweet
Which makes it incomplete
Don't know if it was a trick or treat
The day Cupid decided we should meet

# Deepest Love

Heart to heart
Off the chart
Never to break apart
I knew from the very start

It would be you and me
From your innocent hi
To your gorgeous starry eyes
That it would be the two of us
Until the day we die

No regrets
Nothing to threat
I won a lifetime bet
The day we met

Sweet to the core
Whom I adore
A love like ours
Will never be destroyed

I love waking up to your
Beautiful smiling face
Never to be replaced
To lose you
Would be a disgrace

You have captured my
Mind, body, and soul
For the rest of your life to control
And I have yours to console
Until we're both old

I thank the Lord every day
For sending you my way
Promise to never betray
I'm here to stay
Okay

The deepest love I've ever felt
Makes my heart melt
A true dove
Sent from up above
For only me
To cherish and love

# Diary Love

*If* only I could express my feelings for you
The way I express them in my diary

If only you knew how badly
I wanted to be with you
But for right now only my diary does

You feel for me
And I feel for you

You have another and so do I
Therefore we keep it simple
With a hi and goodbye

I express my every thought of you
In my diary everyday
I wish for once things went my way
You and I could be together
With no consequences to pay

You can read my eyes
And I can read your smile
Our urges growing stronger
For each other all the while

We work hard to conceal our feelings for one another
To prevent from hurting others

Life is not always fair
And we're unaware
Until that special one comes along
And you wish you two were a pair

I'll keep my feelings for you alive in my diary
Until we can be together
Sharing our love in sunshine, rain, or in whatever weather

I'll keep my secret hidden in my written agenda
Since I can't express them to you
If only you knew
Maybe then our dreams would come true
But for right now, my diary will have to do

# Electrifying Emotions

An irresistible attraction and desire from the very start
Can't really describe the feelings that electrified my heart
Constant thoughts of you consuming my brain
Can't focus on anything
Have to be love
**Lust** or **Love** at first sight
I'm thinking love would best describe the way I feel tonight
Never felt like this before with no other
Which is why I'm curious to indulge a little further
Such a deep connection
From two strangers
Eying each other like we're hypnotized
Instant butterflies
Place crowded
But it feels like just us two
In the entire place
The moment I laid eyes upon his face
Everyone else erased
Cupid's arrow didn't fail
This time it prevailed
This feels like a romantic fairytale
And our love is about to set sail
On an incredible journey
Who'd ever think
A perfect stranger would captivate my heart
This time I hit the jackpot
This is not fake
If it is, it's a risk I'm willing to take
Encounters like these are few
And I'm definitely going to pursue
Because meeting my soulmate
Is a dream come true

# Enchanted By You

*W*hen I laid my eyes on you
I was instantly captivated
By your smile
Beautiful teeth and all
Your muscular physique
And the unique dimples in your cheeks

Can't seem to erase your image from my mind
Been a long time since I've been so enthralled
Glad I chose this day to visit the mall

The look you returned
Made my heart burn
And my stomach churned
Felt as though I was about to come undone
Mutual attraction between us was immediately confirmed

Seduced without a touch from your hands
Love at first sight is hard for some to understand
When it's not planned
But my mind, body, and soul
Told me you were my man

I don't care what people say
This is one of my happiest days
So glad our paths crossed
Else, our love for each other
Would have been forever lost

Fate
Sometimes on time
Sometimes comes late
But whatever time it decides to make its presence known
It's well worth the wait
When it sends you your perfect mate

# Good Love

I want good love
I want great love
I want the best love
I want unconditional love

I want the kind of love that drives you out of your mind
The kind that's too irresistible to leave behind
The kind that only every blue moon you'll find

The kind that sends chills up and down your spine
The kind that makes you think your man is super fine
The kind that gives you a buzz without drinking wine

The kind you want to share with the world
The kind that makes your toes curl
The kind that has you acting like a little
Spoiled boy or girl

The kind that keeps a permanent smile upon your face
The kind that wins your heart at first base
The kind that can never be replaced

The kind that makes you want to act wild
The kind that makes you want to have a child

The kind that you wish would last and last
The kind that's a blast
The kind that makes your days go by fast
The kind that makes you forget about your past

The kind where you started out as best friends
The kind that's not fake or pretend
The kind that stays strong from beginning to end

That's the kind of love I'd recommend!

# If I Give My Love

*I*f I give you my love
What will you do with it?
Will you honor it?
Will you cherish it?
Will you give yours in return?
For us to learn
Each other
In depth
My heart
Your heart
Us from the start
I need you
You need me
Respect and treasure
Our feelings
Love unconditionally
Just you and me
Together for eternity
You be there for me
And I'll be there for you
Do whatever we have to do
To keep our love alive
Make it thrive
Never deprive
With you right by my side
As my ever-loving bride
Till death do us part
Baby, I'll love you until my heart
**Stops!**

# Hanging In There For Love

For the love we once shared
Now the love only one possesses
My love remains the same
Your love somehow lost its flame
Don't really know who's to blame

I don't want to give up
I still believe we can make it work
Still believe we can get back on track
Improving the love one of us lacks

It's just a temporary distraction
Just need to pump up the interaction
To stimulate an attraction
To your satisfaction

My love is strong enough to carry us both
Through this period of turmoil
I'll be here to console
Until we're once again made whole

I have so many reasons to stay
And not let the love of my life get stolen away
For better or worse, vows I tend to obey
Our love is too deep to throw away

Open up your eyes
Listen to your heart
Search your inner soul
Reminisce about the love
We once controlled

I'm here for you until the end
Here until what ails you mends
Here until your love transcends
Here for life
For my wife
My lover
My best friend!

# Just Us 2

When there's nothing left
I know I will still have you
Our love for one another
Everlasting
Surpassing
Till the end of time

A love so strong
It rights the wrongs
Our love is so amazing
A testament that we belong

I'll always be here for you
And you for me
So glad there's no price tag
Love is free
You're the only gift I'll ever want
Underneath my Christmas tree

True love is indescribable
Such a high
Two hearts intertwined
Blowing each other's mind
There's nothing of its kind

Two hearts mended into one
Never to come undone
Enjoying each other and having fun

I pray we never depart
Until the day we die
Want to be right next to you in and after life
Forever as your loving wife

# Keep Going Back

*I* don't know why I keep going back
Setting myself up for another vicious attack
Forcing me to pack

Acting like he's the only guy
Can't find the words to tell him good-bye
I continue to stay, enduring more lies

The chemistry between us is so deep
Still love him when he acts like a creep
His love swept me off of my feet

Wished I had the strength to leave
Wished I could learn to breathe
Wished I could learn not to grieve
Wished I wasn't so naive

Everyone keep asking why I stay
Why I let him treat me this away
I keep telling them I will leave one day
It's the only thing I can manage to say

My heart can't take being apart
Even though the decision to stay isn't smart

I can't help that I'm in love with the wrong man
Only if you've ever truly been deeply in love will you understand
The love command
It's not as easy as you think
Letting go of your lover hand
When you utterly love a man

Roberta Blango

# Love You Like There's No Tomorrow

Never in life experienced a love like this
Heart constantly filled with bliss
Ever since our first kiss
Never knew this kind of love
Even exists

Love at first sight
This time I got it right
Snuggled in your loving arms
Every night

I'm going to love only you
For the rest of my life
You are a dream come true
Promise to always be there
No matter what ups and downs
We may go through

A real man indeed
Pleasuring my every need
Baby, you're a rare breed
One hundred percent
Guaranteed

Just one glance
And I was in a trance
So glad I took a chance
For this once in a lifetime
Loving romance

You are my all in all
Will always be here when you call
Catch you when you fall

I'm going to love you
Like there's no tomorrow
Because tomorrow is not promised to us
So we must
Live and love each other with all our might
From dawn to dust
For the rest of our lives
If I ever lose you
My heart would truly be
Forever crushed

# Love Songs

Love songs can be so meaningful
Make you reminisce
Fill your heart with bliss
Take you on a journey
Back in time
To visit the good old days
When everything was good
Happy go lucky
Nothing standing in your way
Nothing could ruin your day
Heart free
Too blind
To foresee any future misery
Pop on that love song
To put you in the mood
Make you forget about someone being rude
Touches your inner soul
Love takes control
Of your every being
So when you're feeling down
Pop one on
And start feeling good again

# One & Only

$\mathcal{E}$veryone's desire is to be....
The **One** and **Only** to capture that special one's heart
Praying never to depart
Hoping for a connection so strong
It belongs in a love song
Eyes for only you
Feelings one hundred percent true
That gentle brush across your face
That incredible smile never to erase
Whispering sweet nothings in your ear
Causing happy tears
To roll down your cheeks
Making your entire body weak
Unable to speak
Never want it to end
Want the love to transcend
Till the test of time
Possibility of it ending would be a crime
Hoping they continue choosing only you
Until the day you both say I do
Representing true love still exists
With that one and only precious kiss!

# Pains & Pleasures of Love

A thin line separates the two
Depends on who you give your heart to
Depends on if he/she really loves you
In the beginning it's full of pleasure because it's new
Then three months later you'll find out if it's really true
Could turn out good
Or turn out to be someone you thought you knew

It's a game we all must play
It's all up to you if they go or stay
Love is like a freeway
Some days it's smooth
Some days constant delays
Stuck with no throughway

Love can trick the mind
Make one blind
Make one forget all about the pain
As soon as pleasure enters the scene
It's a physical connection that can't be explained

The heart is untamed
Can't be framed
Only a few able to claim
What a shame

One of the reasons why true love is so hard to find
The heart is like a maze
Intertwined
To explore and blow one's mind
A complicated design

Makes one happy or sad
Cry or laugh
Bringing joy or sorrow
Forever more
Down to the core
Of
The pains and pleasures of love

# Respect Love

*I*'ve learned the value of true love
The love that folks dream of
The love actors display on TV
The love you rarely see
The love that's now a part of me

The love you only experience once in a lifetime
The love that drives you out of your mind
The love that makes you blind
The love you don't ever want to leave behind

The love that keeps a permanent smile upon your face
The love you want no others to invade your space
The love you constantly embrace

The love you've built from scratch
The love that was hard to match
The love that was ultimately the perfect catch

A love that's divine
A love that's forever mine
From someone who's
Honest, sweet, gentle, and kind

# Till Death Do Us Part

*I*'m here for the long run
Even when we feel the love coming undone
And it's no longer fun
And we both weigh a ton
You'll still be the only one I want to call my hun

I'll forgive you if you mess up
And I hope you will do the same
I want you to forever bear my last name
Because marriage is not a game
We'll be fine if we stay on the commitment team

Want to enjoy summer vacations with you
Want to grow old with you
Go through trial and tribulations with you
Enjoy raising kids with you
All the fun things married couples do

You were a sight for sore eyes
The first day I saw you
I knew
I would spend the rest of my life with you
And thank God my dream came true
Through thick and thin
I will forever only
**Love You**!

# True Love

True love develops from the depths of one's soul
To love until you're both old
That special one you can't wait to hold
Keeping that love alive is the ultimate goal

Through good times and bad
Sick or well
Rich or poor
Homeless and starving
He or she will still remain your darling

Come rain
Sunshine
Or
Snow
Hold on tight
Never let go

Through tears of pain
Tears of joy
Tears you've yet to explore
Love concurs all for sure

Share your thoughts
Share your dreams
And a future unforeseen

AS

Husband and wife
Partners for life

# Without Love

Without love
You don't have much
Because without love
You have nothing
Love is what keeps us sane
Love controls your brain
Love is number one in the game
Above it all
Love
Is a popular thing
It's here, there, and everywhere
It's what two or more share
Runs up and down your veins
Makes one want to scream
In pleasurable pain
Draining
Your mind
Your body
Your soul
Conquer it
Once or twice
However many times
Just make it your goal
To experience this amazing gift
The Lord has a place in each
And everyone one of us
It comes natural
Don't have to be forced
Or
You'll end up in a divorce
Don't let true love pass you by
Before you die

We All

S
t
r
e
s
s

# Explode

*I* feel like my head is about to explode
All this chaos disturbing my brain
Tears streaming down my face
Wishing my problems would erase

Crazy thoughts enter my mind
But I stop at the thought of leaving
Loved ones behind

There's only so much a person can take
Everyone needs a break
Before they break
Leaving family and friends
Full of sadness at their wake

Just when things are going good
All hell breaks loose
Leaving you struggling like an oil tortured goose
Making you want to drown your sorrows with booze

Anything to take the pain away
Anything to see a better day
Anything to make it okay
Anything to delay
This dismay

I need a special healing
To cure this feeling
Inside my soul
Making me feel cold
I need help to escape
This black hole

It's pulling me deeper and deeper
I need my heavenly keeper
To protect me from the grand reaper

It's hard to elude his sneaky tricks
You must think quick
Because he's extra slick
Leaving you mentally sick

It's going to take a lot of praying
And obeying
We all suffer from one thing or another
But He hears our call
And He'll help us stand when we fall
Because He guarantees to give his **All** and **All**
When His children call

# Inner Pain

Inner pain
Is often disguised
With a beautiful smile
On the outside
To hide
One's real feelings
Due to someone
Not willing or ready to deal
So they smile and chill
Act as though their problem is no big deal
While on the inside
They're about to explode
Due to the overwhelming load
They refuse to expose
They'd rather keep their secrets enclosed
Don't want folks to impose
Don't want to hear what they have to say
At least not right away
Maybe one day
But for now...
The secrets stay buried down deep
For safe keep
Will continue to endure the pain
Consuming their brain
About to make them go insane
If only someone could hear their inner screams
Things would change
Making life better
Pain diminished
Their inner soul replenished
But that won't happen
Until they are ready to share
Or until a family member becomes aware
One who really cares

Who can read between the lines of their blank stare
Finally!
Help arrives to make that pain take a dive
And their soul revived
So they can once again feel alive
And not deprived
By all that inner pain
Welcome back
Self-esteem!

# State of Depression

*I* feel like my life is going in the wrong direction
So many things need correcting

If I could get paid for all the tears
That have traveled down my cheeks
I'd be rich

One devastating disappointment after the next
My life is becoming more and more complex

I want to be free from all this mess
Free from stress
Want my heart to ache less
Along with all the rest

Encountering so many trials
Waiting for things to turn around
Waiting to be lifted up off the ground
Waiting for there to be no more frowns

This too shall pass
It won't continue to last
Because I got down on my knees and asked

The Lord,
For a better day
For him to guide my way
For him to take all the pain away
He promised everything will be okay

I trust and I believe
In the blessing I'm about to receive
Because our Lord and Savior,
Never deceives

# Stress Mess

*T*oo much stress
Can't handle all this mess
I need some rest

One thing happening after the next
Can't seem to catch a break
My anxiety is driving me insane
Hard coping with so many things

My entire livelihood at risk
Due to my own stupidity
I'm so pissed

One devastating mistake
Is what it took for me to awake
And causing my family so much heartbreak

I'm trying to turn things around
Standing my ground
Due to the much needed help I found

Everyone needs a helping hand
When they can no longer stand
To handle all life's incredible demands

What really matters is
I'm now on the right track
To getting my life back
There are times when we all slack

I'll be better prepared for my next trial
This experience was all worthwhile
A lesson learned
Respect for life earned

This stress
Turned me into a hot mess
But I was blessed
Got help to get me through this process
And thanks to God, it has been a success

# Stressful Situations

Stress overtaking my mind
Peace unable to find
Life sometimes seems so unkind
Especially when the problems are combined

Every time things appear to be fine
You tend to trip over life's "I gotcha again" line
Dragging you back into depression
As soon as your head gets above the recession

You start to feel doomed
Don't want to talk on the phone
Just want to be alone
To think things through on your own

You ask yourself
What am I doing wrong?
Trial after trial all life long
But you have no choice
But to remain strong

You will eventually bounce back
Getting on track
Once more
Praying that these dreadful trials
Stay away from your door

We all go through life's trials
Some a little
Others a lot
Doesn't matter your lifestyle
Everyone gets caught

You have to pray it away
Try to enjoy your day
Stressing won't help your situation
The Lord will send you inspiration
To end your frustration

# The Blues

The blues
The blues
The sad sad blues
Over some bad news
Or someone who refused
Or maybe someone that got used
Or wearing too little shoes
Or you couldn't figure out some important clues
Or you're tired of people who constantly sue
Or you're sick of long drive-thrus
Or maybe drank too much booze
Or maybe missed your cruise
Or maybe got a scrap or bruise
Or didn't have money to pay your dues
Or someone left you confused
Or didn't like someone's point of views
Or someone disrupted your snooze,
And you got mad and blew a fuse,
And needed to be defused
Or your bad luck came in twos
Or you were wrongly accused
Or didn't like your tattoos,
And wasn't enthused
Or you want to win and never lose
Or just depressed by world news
Or you're sick with a cold or flu,
Making your nose ooze
Or mad because there aren't enough zoos
Or maybe you don't like the word **Or** being overused
And this poem didn't leave you amused
I don't know which statement applies to you,
You choose

# Things Come Undone

There will be a time in your life when things come undone
And it's no longer fun
Making you want to jump up and run,
Away!

But they will follow
Some situations are hard to swallow
And can't be bottled,
Up!

Doesn't matter how hard you try
To pretend
They don't exist

Some will drive you crazy
Some will drain you and make you lazy
Some will have you feeling hazy

But remember, you're not alone
To deal with this on your own
Just because you're grown
Swallow your pride and pick up the phone

We can all use a caring ear
To guide and help us persevere
When our lives become disarrayed and unclear
You should always keep a friend or family member near

A mess, a hot mess
Can cause so much unnecessary stress
Eliminating much needed rest

*Roberta Blango*

You must go on and not let it consume you
You must force it out of your brain
Or your days left on earth will be few

Make the right choice
Listen to that positive inner voice
Start living your life to the fullest and rejoice

# Uprooted Life

Life's changes
Sometimes the strangest
Experiences to endure
Some pure
Some not so sure
But whatever ails you
There's always a cure

Some remedy to bring you through
What's happening to you
You're not alone
So many others going through the same mess
Overwhelming stress
Endlessly depressed

Trying to find a way out
Way to escape
To some form of comfort and peace
To try and release
All the things crowding your mind
Hoping to soon unwind

Temporary it may be
A life filled with uncertainty
If you don't possess the master key
This repeating is a possibility

Never expect what you don't know
It's a mystery
Until it comes to be
For you to see

*Roberta Blango*

Take life one day at a time
Take it in stride
Take it with a sense of pride
No one is born with a life's user guide

Feel your way through
There will be a bump or two
But you'll pull through
Like you always manage to do

Uprooted lives
Can be replanted
As long as you don't
Take it for granted

We All

S

u

f

f

e

r

From Heartbreak

# Broken

$\mathcal{Y}$ou've crushed my inner self
And I have nothing left
Because of your degrading
And ranting and raving

I let you enter my head
Wishing I was dead
Should have left you instead
You're the one thing in my life
I most dread

You broke me
But I finally escaped
Your constant abuse

I'm free
Now that I'm away from you
I no longer hate myself
I love me

I know now
That you never loved me
Real love never hurt
You made me feel less than dirt

Pain is all I ever felt with you
Day and night
I knew it wasn't right
But you had me brainwashed
And thank God I discovered the light

*Roberta Blango*

But thank you
It was a lesson learned
To prepare myself from ever again
Getting burned
By a guy like you
Ruthless and unconcerned

In life you have to know
When to stay, go, or run
If you don't want your life
To come undone
Take it from me
It's no fun

# Damage Done

The damage is done
I want out
We've had our fun
We gave it a good run

The time has come for us to depart
No love left in either of our hearts

Time for you to go your way
And me to go my way
This burden can no longer be delayed

There's no respect left between us
This separation is a must

You want it to end as well as me
We've finally found something on which we can both agree

Friendship is not an option
If I ever see you again, I'll speak

That's better for both
Continuing to see one another
Will only stunt our growth

Let's reminisce about the good times
Forget about the bad times
And laugh about this when we're well in our prime

We gave it our best
Our problems have been addressed
Let's go our merry ways
And forget about all the rest

# I'm Happy 4 U

It hurt that you didn't choose me
But nevertheless I'm happy for you two
Hopefully I'll find someone like you

Thought we were doing good
Don't know why you didn't express
What had you so stressed?
You were the best
It just wasn't meant to be I guess

I loved you so much
The split took me by surprise
At first I **despised** you
But you had to do
What you had to do

Now you're marrying someone you just met
And I haven't even gotten over you yet
But I wish you the best
But I must confess
The news ripped my heart right out of my chest

Another lesson learned
After you're at the point of no return
And getting burned
But for your love I still yearn

My heart shattered into a million pieces
But somehow I managed to mend it back together
With no regrets, no harsh feelings
I love you too much to hate you
You will always be my first love

Thought we could remain friends
Sorry, but it's too hard
We should have never crossed the friendship line
Now I've lost you for good and you're no longer mine
We will rekindle our friendship in time

Don't know what I did wrong
Don't know if it was something I said
I must stop wrecking my head
My heart was misled
By my best friend taking me to bed

# I'm So Broken

So broken
Inside and out
My heart aches
Some days
Don't want to awake
To the same ole bull
Can't be my destiny
A life of misery
No joy
Constant blues
No happy days
Ever comes my way
So lost
Want to be found
Instead of constantly
Wearing a frown
When will this agony
Turn around
So many wasted years
Worthless tears
The pain
Driving me insane
**So broken**
Don't know
If another
Will ever
Be able
To repair
This damage
Tall as the

Empire State Building
I'm incredibly numb
Will take
Years of healing
To regain my feelings
Until then
I'll be chilling
ALONE!

# It's Me

It's been a while but not that long
This sudden amnesia seems wrong
You're making me want to listen to a sad love song

All those precious moments we spent together
In all types of weather
I feel like telling you to forget me forever

Can't believe I had to jog your memory of me
This is a day I thought I'd never foresee
I'm going to record this in my diary

To remind myself never to be fooled again
By you or any other man
This heartbreak wasn't a part of my plans

I thought we'd stroll down memory lane
Not you inflicting so much pain
Acting lame, you're not the same
Was it all just a game?

You probably never wanted me from the start
Just going around breaking hearts
Wish I knew martial arts

I'd teach you a lesson
So you'd stop messing
Causing unnecessary stressing

Everything happens for a reason
Guess this wasn't my season

Love will eventually find me
Or I'll find it
As soon as I learn to recommit
And you split

# I've Been a Fool

I've been a fool for you
Letting you take advantage of my heart
Letting you rule my every move
My every thought
So blinded by my love for you
A love that only I possess
Because you've proved
That you could care less
Over and over again
But still I stayed
Although on so many occasions
Feeling low and betrayed
My self-esteem vanished
Into thin air
Turning my life into a nightmare
With all of your affairs
But I kept the faith
Kept hoping
You'd soon change
You'd soon get over this stage
Get over all your rage
Get over treating me like
An animal in a cage
You never did
It got worse
I can only take but so much
You showed me
You didn't have to tell me
Actions do speak louder than words
I'm leaving you
My heart can't take this anymore
I still love you
But I know now
You don't feel the same

*Roberta Blango*

I'm not going to remain your fool
One day you're going to wake up
And realize
You've lost a true jewel
And regret how you treated me
So cruel

# Love Gone Away

Love doesn't live in my heart anymore
I gave it once and it was destroyed
And left an empty void

I don't want it back
My soul is pitch black
From the love attack
The love, I now lack

It destroyed my brain
Drove me insane
And caused the worst kind of pain

I never knew there was a hole so deep
A place where broken hearts go to weep
Caused by some worthless creep

It hurt so immensely when you've given your best
And you stay stressed
Because you know the one you're with could care less
Loving someone who no longer loves you is hard to digest

I thought a love so strong would never end
Especially when we were best friends
This unexpected departure was hard to comprehend

I did everything right
Always calm and polite
Food served hot every night
Tried to keep a smile on his face bright
How could our love ignite?

I never thought true love would not be enough
Finding out he was a cheater was rough
Still, letting go was tough

Without trust, a relationship is dead
You might as well be alone and happy instead

I hurt
Felt less than dirt
Thought our love was true
But the joke was on me
I didn't have a clue
Of the person I thought I knew

# Loveless

Don't stay because of the kids
Don't stay because of the house
Don't stay because of the bills
Don't stay because you feel sorry
Don't stay, leave if you no longer love me

Staying will only cause me more pain
Because your feelings for me are not the same
Your excuses are getting lamer
I wish this whole mess was all a dream

You promised to love me for life
The day you made me your wife
Your infidelity is like getting stabbed over and over
By an extremely sharp machete knife

How could you allow another to come in between
I don't know this person you've become,
Treating me so mean
I was once your only queen

Get out and go your own way
I can no longer live this life we portray
Dishonoring your vows day by day
Continuing to betray
I don't want you to stay

I never thought I'd be getting a divorce
But you've given me no other choice

I'm setting you free
So you don't have to sneak around trying to avoid me
I'm the one who will have the last laugh, I guarantee

The kids and I will be just fine
Even they got tired of your lying
Breaking promises, leaving them crying
This marriage is officially over
Because I'm tired trying

**Goodbye!**

# Love's A Beast

*C*an't eat
Can't sleep
Can't focus
Don't know what to do
This is what love puts one through
If it's true
Love......

Feel like the world is coming to an end
Feel like you've lost your best friend
A broken heart is hard to mend

Cry to ease the pain
Drink to distract your brain
Pray in hopes the relationship will remain

Become obsessed
Downright depressed
Turn into a hot mess
Because the love of your life
Ripped your heart out of your chest

Some are blind to it
Some see it coming
Some don't care that their lover
Is having an affair
As long as they remain a pair

You blame yourself
That your mate left
When someone tries to tell you otherwise
You act deaf

*Roberta Blango*

A broken heart takes time to heal
Especially the one who got a raw deal
But you must have a strong will
Swallow and dispose that love pill
In preparation for someone that's real

You will find someone new
To take away your blues
And who will truly love
You too

# Saddest Day

The saddest day of my life
Is when you walked out that door
Telling me you don't love me anymore
And you wanted to explore

Thought I would die
You telling me goodbye
Couldn't stop the tears falling from my eyes

A hole as big as the Grand Canyon
In my heart
I sunk deeper than the deepest sea
When you left me

How could you destroy my joy?
Thought we were happy
Thought I was all you ever wanted
All you ever needed
How could you deceive me?

I could never love another
The way I loved you
Now you're telling me we're through
Tell me it's not true

I don't want anyone
If I can't have you
Please take me back
I feel like I'm about to crack

Can't control the dark thoughts in my head
Since you left my bed
Can't get over the harsh things you said
Can't believe how my feeling was misled

By your dishonesty
Constantly lying to me
Telling me for the rest of our lives
It would only be you and me

This is the worst day
But I'm going to be okay
Go play
But when you get tired
Don't even **think** about coming back my way

# Shame Game

So, so, ashamed
I've caused such pain
No longer want you to complain
I promise to change

Sad teary face
No welcomed embrace
Hearts been displaced
Love erased

I caused this mess
Unnecessary stress
Now that I've confessed
This relationship will be blessed
I'm going to let the Lord
Handle the rest

I'll do my part
To try and restart
By regaining your trust
Sit down and discuss
My unjust

Clear the air
Forgiving shows you still care
The Lord answered my prayers
You made me aware
That a love like ours is rare

Thanks
For taking me back
After the shameful way I've acted
Precious as you are
I know I've left a lasting scar

I'll make it up to you for the rest of my life
To endure such strife
And continue to love
I couldn't find another
Beautiful, devoted, and exquisite
As you my darling wife

# That Sad Look

That sad expression upon my face
Tells a sob story of blue
Although I attempt to cover it up
To fool you

The eyes don't lie
Even when one tries
The sadness can't be disguised
When it comes to a broken heart
That's been compromised

The long droopy face
Upside down smile
Spaced out stare
Feeling that no one cares

Trying to hold back the tears
Trying to forget about all the years
Trying to stir my mind clear
As the signs of breakup sparks fears
And knowing the end is near

Want to be happy in the worst way
Knowing breaking up will ultimately be my happiest day
I must keep telling myself I'm going to be okay
But not if I continue to stay

I want to turn this sad face into joy
A smile so wide
Want to show all my teeth
Want this pain to escape way down beneath
Where I constantly hide it

*Roberta Blango*

Tired of settling for less
Tired of living life stressed
Knowing I'm not doing my best
All these years and nothing progressed
It's my time to be happy like the rest

A lesson learned
A quest I've yearned
Its way overdue for my life to take a
Ninety degree turn

# Whatta Ya Doing

*I*'m so confused
And feeling used
And emotionally abused

Why are you playing with my head?
After visiting my bed
Stop acting like a boy
Be a man instead

You either want me
Or you don't

Stop treating me like you don't care
Don't want your friends to be aware
That you and I are a pair

If you don't want anyone to know
Then I'll go
But I refuse to let you treat me like a ho

I treat you with respect
And I deserve the same
I don't have time for childish games

Love me or leave me
But don't deceive me
Because you wouldn't like
The old me
Believe me

Don't break my heart
If this is fake
I'd rather depart

So tell me now
And not later
Your friends are just being haters

I love you
You said you loved me too
So give it to me straight
Are we going to be together
Or are we through?

# Why Must I

Why must I continue to endure so much pain?
Torturing my brain
Driving me insane

Why must I be punished with dismay?
Nothing going my way
Life in disarray

Can't seem to get it together
Thought it would get better
Wrong again
Time to break free of this chain

Why must I allow others to suffer?
Enough is enough
Of this petty stuff

Can't change a persons' ways
Wasted so many days
Time to do the right thing
Try to fly with one wing

I ask why, why, why
Must I
Now it's time for me to try

This can't be my fate
Bite off the wrong bait
Hope it's not too late
For my true soulmate

*Roberta Blango*

I will keep hope alive
Stop feeling deprived
Until something new arrives

Nothing lasts forever
It will soon be over
You live and you learn
No more asking why
Must I
Live life sadly
Slowly passing me by

# You Blew My Mind

*I* was praying that the rumor wasn't true
After all we've been through
I can't believe you had the heart
To dump me like I meant nothing to you

She's just a baby
You left me for a child
How could you do this?
What did I miss?
This was an unexpected twist
Occurring right after our wedding bliss

All our years together down the drain
Because you started thinking with the wrong brain
You should be ashamed
Playing such childish games

Grow up and be a man
You need to act your age
You're beyond that immature stage
Now I hear you two are engaged

My head dropped
My ears popped
My heart stopped
I couldn't move
As though my legs
Had been chopped

Tears streamed
Intense pain
Flooded my brain

Felt like I was about to go insane
My composure, I could not regain
My marriage was over
And I didn't even know this little girl's name

This hurt to the third degree
Never thought in a million years
You'd ever leave me
I guess it wasn't meant to be
I have no choice but to set you free

Love can damage your mind
Make you treat people unkind
Leave your soul confined
Make you want to stay behind
An enclosed door
Because sometimes it's just
Not worth fighting for
Anymore!

# Your Sadness

The sadness in your eyes
Can't be disguised
I can easily recognize
And I empathize
You don't find this in too many guys

A sensitive side
Heart opened wide
Swallowing your pride
You let your feelings show
And it's well justified

A broken heart hurts
Makes one feel less than dirt
Now I understand why
You were being such an introvert
Ignoring my persistent flirt

I want to help ease your pain
Uplift your self esteem
By first, you telling me your name
You're so cute
Whoever broke your heart
Should be ashamed

I'd like to turn that frown
Upside down
With a beautiful smile
Promise I'll make it worthwhile

I'll revive your wounded heart
With a new spark
Erasing your stress marks
Let's start with a refreshing
Stroll in the park

You no longer have to cry
Or ask why
I'm here for you to rely
So tell those hurtful memories
Goodbye

I'll never let you go
I'm here to stay
It's hard for you to comprehend that now
But you'll realize it one day
I mean what I say
It's no cliché
I'll never lead you astray or betray
Okay!

We've All

E
x
p
e
r
i
e
n
c
e
d

Sadness

# Cherish the Ones You Love

*O*ne of the saddest days
Is when a loved one passes away
And you have no control to make them stay
Nothing you can do or say

Never again to see their smiling face
They're gone without a trace
Out of this place
Presence forever erased

All you're left with is memories to cherish
Now that they've perished

Enjoy your loved ones while you can
In the blink of an eye
They can die
Leaving you asking why

When your number is up
It's nothing you or anyone else can do
But feel the blues
Over losing you

Embrace the ones you love
By putting them above
The petty stuff
Because they are deserving of
Not part, but all your love

# Mighty Attack (9/11)

Nine-eleven was so destructive
So many innocent lives destroyed
But now they're in the mighty hands of our Lord

Cowards, the names of their assailants
Cold, ruthless, and heartless
To the third degree
But they'll one day answer to a higher power
I guarantee

They didn't have a chance
Gone in the blink of an eye
Didn't imagine it would be the day they'd die
Didn't even get an opportunity
To tell their loved ones good-bye

One of the saddest days in America
Everyone shed tears of their loss
Whether they were
Family, friends, or just volunteers
The devastation of nine-eleven will continue
To haunt us for years

It was a vicious act hard to swallow
I pray to God there will never be another to follow
Here today, gone tomorrow
Leaving so many hearts hollow

They can never be replaced
As defined on the expressions of their loved ones faces
Even though they know they're at peace in a safer place
Full of God's loving grace

# Take Me With U

*I* loved my wife so much
I wanted to die with her
Be buried with her
I can't go on without her
The love of my life
I wanted to depart from this earth
With my sweet loving wife

There is no other for me
No one could ever take her place
Our memories together
Will never be erased
From my mind
My every thought
Why did my darling leave me behind?

I've never been so lonely and sad
Felt so bad
For fifty years
This sweet woman was all I had
So yes, I'm mad

Why was she taken away?
Why couldn't the Lord delay?
Her stay
For just one more minute, hour, or day
I didn't get an opportunity to say
A word to my baby
Before she went to heaven on her merry way

*Roberta Blango*

I can't take this pain
Inside my brain
I wanted someone to blame
My life will never be the same

Lord, take me too please
I'm the one with a heart disease
Take my heart and squeeze
The life out so I can lie beside my wife
Then my soul will be at ease

# Where Are You

$S$ix feet under
How can that be
You were just here with me

Didn't get to tell you good-bye
You were gone in the blink of an eye
Leaving me to mourn and cry

Didn't even know you were sick
The news hit me like a ton of bricks

I'm going to miss you so very bad
As I sit reminiscing about the fun times we had
Why did you leave me, Dad

You were all I had left
Now I'm here all by myself

I wish you were still here
To whisper I love you in my ears
And to take away my fears

Dad, I know one day I'll see you again
I'll join you and Mom
And we will walk in heaven together
Hand in hand

*We may live worlds apart from one another,*
*but at some point in our lives,*

**We are**

S
I
M
U
L
T
A
N
E
O
U
S
L
Y

IN

E
X
I
S
T
E
N
C
E